T0334709

Cambridge Elements ≡

Elements in Religion and Violence
edited by
Margo Kitts
Hawai'i Pacific University
Founding Editor
†James R. Lewis
Wuhan University

VIOLENCE AND RELIGIOUS CHANGE IN THE PACIFIC ISLANDS

Garry Trompf
University of Sydney

CAMBRIDGE
UNIVERSITY PRESS

Shaftesbury Road, Cambridge CB2 8EA, United Kingdom

One Liberty Plaza, 20th Floor, New York, NY 10006, USA

477 Williamstown Road, Port Melbourne, VIC 3207, Australia

314–321, 3rd Floor, Plot 3, Splendor Forum, Jasola District Centre, New Delhi – 110025, India

103 Penang Road, #05–06/07, Visioncrest Commercial, Singapore 238467

Cambridge University Press is part of Cambridge University Press & Assessment, a department of the University of Cambridge.

We share the University's mission to contribute to society through the pursuit of education, learning and research at the highest international levels of excellence.

www.cambridge.org
Information on this title: www.cambridge.org/9781009094047

DOI: 10.1017/9781009091336

First published 2023

A catalogue record for this publication is available from the British Library.

ISBN 978-1-009-09404-7 Paperback
ISSN 2397-9496 (online)
ISSN 2514-3786 (print)

Violence and Religious Change in the Pacific Islands

Elements in Religion and Violence

DOI: 10.1017/9781009091336

First published online: July 2023

Garry Trompf
University of Sydney

Author for correspondence: Garry Trompf, garry.trompf@sydney.edu.au

ABSTRACT: This Element considers patterns of violent behaviour among the inhabitants of the Pacific Islands while their vast region has been undergoing religious change, overwhelmingly towards Christianity. Major topics researched are religion-based violent reactions to early intruders (including missionaries); new religious movements resisting unwanted interference (including 'cargo cults'); anti-colonial rebellions inspired by spiritual impetuses both indigenous and introduced; and the persistence of traditional modes of violence (tribal fighting, sorcery and tough punishments) adapted to altered conditions.

KEYWORDS: violence, religion, Oceania, social change, cargo cults

ISBNs: 9781009094047 (PB), 9781009091336 (OC)
ISSNs: 2397-9496 (online), 2514-3786 (print)

Contents

1 Background to the Study of Socio-Religious Change in the Pacific Islands

Over a fifth of our planet's discrete tradional religions arose among the Pacific Islands, between the Bird's Head (Vogelkop) at the far western reaches of New Guinea and Easter Island (or Rapanui) far out in the eastern Pacific Ocean. With interactions between violence and religion to the forefront, this Element surveys the repercussions of outside contact on this vast region during modern times, from the earliest landfalls of European explorers to the establishment of colonies by foreign powers, and on to the emergence of independent nations (see Fig. 1). In virtually all the 1,340-odd endogenous Pacific Islander cultures of the past, warriorhood was cultivated for group survival and became integral to total lifeways (Trompf 2021a). Over the last two centuries, however, massive socio-religious change has occurred, with more extensive foreign-generated trading networks, plantations, mining, capitalist development, urbanism and modern political organizations. Alongside these secular processes, and often ambiguously placed towards them, missionary activity has altered the whole region's religious profile, which is registered today as 92 per cent Christian. This immense socio-religious transformation is usually acknowledged to have brought a sustainable peace to Oceania; but matters to do with the human propensity for violence are never simple and this Element seeks to address the complexities. The many external impacts hardly came without brutal coercion and produced violent retaliations by Islanders in return. Colonial administrative rules and Church standards of behavioural conformity, intended to 'pacify' localized warrior ferocities, did not have their grip without reactivity (Rodman and Cooper 1983). Innovative religious responses, mixing tradition and Christianity, could entail violent 'reprisal', and eventually spiritual ideals bolstered anti-colonial 'rebellions' (Trompf 2008a: 162–232, 350–55). And local pre-contact impetuses towards violent solutions still hung on, especially in Melanesia – the most complicated ethnologic scene on earth – where the pace of adjustments was slower and where tribal warfare has been exacerbated by new weaponry.

While reckoning with forms of violence entailed by foreigners' impositions of change, this Element concentrates overwhelmingly on the religious

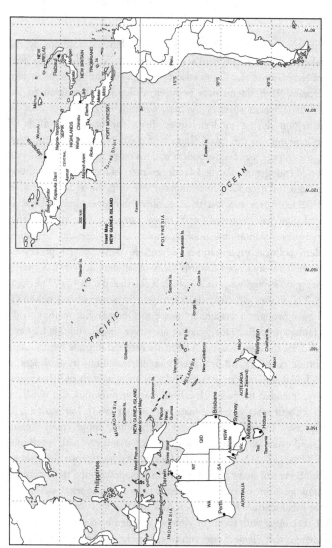

Figure 1 Map of the Pacific Islands

attitudes and acts of Pacific *Islander indigenes*, and (in building upon a companion Element, Trompf 2021a) focuses on their expressions of *physical* violence (rather than those psycho-spiritual or structural in nature) (cf. Stewart and Strathern 2002a). The author has to brave out the embarrassment of assessing measures of violence among peoples outside his own cultural inheritance, yet it will become plain that the key purpose is to offer a broad perspective serviceable for their better solving of present and future social problems. To acquire historical bearings is crucial for our task, and the Element will be organized diachronically, from contact to contemporary affairs, highly informed by the methods and writings of Pacific history. It will also tend to move from anthropological toward sociological concerns, yet remain multidisciplinary (with the history of ideas and religions always opening up possibilities to air ethico-evaluative, pastoral and missiological insights). General differences in social organization across the islands shall be borne in mind. Most of Melanesia is highly variegated in its languages and social structuring, but through widespread Austronesian (or Malay-Polynesian) culturo-linguistic connections, running along Melanesia's edges and into the broad Pacific, distinguishable features of social stratification or chiefly rule over commoners still affect religious life (Terrell 1988). In contrast, strict seniority systems such as those found in these regions (based on the first beachings by canoe) do not apply to hundreds of land-locked cultures, mostly in New Guinea's mountainous interior, where there were not only more egalitarian forms of social control but inclinations to image the cosmos horizontally rather than in Austronesian vertically oriented perspectives (Swain and Trompf 1995: 7–8, 140–5). After contact, Austronesian hierarchies of cosmic and social power have often determined formal religious change from the top, mostly in the nineteenth century, whereas the changes that have resulted from Melanesia's intensely tribal volalities, which are still going on, yield no easy generalization. Daunted by both awkwardness of focus and intricacies of data, the challenge still invites in its importance more than it deters.

How can we best orient ourselves to understand changing patterns of violence and religion among Pacific Islanders in modern times? By 1513, proverbially, *conquistador* Vasco de Balboa had waded into the great South Sea off Panama, and with a sword in his right hand and a Virgin

Mary pennant in his left he declared the waters taken for Spain. If through this pretentious drama the horizonless Mar del Sur was deemed a 'Spanish lake', eight years later, after a fleet from Spain under the Portuguese Ferdinand Magellan had edged around the southern extents of South America and spent ninety-nine long days in calm waters before reaching Guam, 'Oceano Pacifico' became the preferred epithet (Spate 2004: 25–47). In common imagination, the immense region now generally lives up to its name, a zone without incessant tension, full of ideal holiday destinations, quiet towns lolling along to the pace of gentle string-band music or periodically calmed by uplifting surges of hymn-singing. While trouble spots are occasionally reported in worldwide press releases, and by-now-worrying instances of fearful cyclones, the general impression holds that Indigenous Pacific populations (10.65 million Melanesians, 2.2 million Polynesians, 535,000 Micronesians) inhabit 13 independent nations, and 17 special-relation, dependent-island or externally colonized territories, in relative stability and peace (Crocombe 2008). So decidedly Christian do the Islands generally present, albeit within frameworks of traditional lifeways, that those old European stereotypes of dangerous natives, headhunting and savagery have all but disappeared (Meijl and Miedema 2004). Missionary books about 'camping among cannibals' (St. Johnston 1889), or philosophic defences of a universal humanity because 'the Papuan is also a man, not a beast' (Husserl (1936) 1970: 290), are today few and far between. The 'New Time', as common village discourse goes, has obviously replaced the 'Old' (Tomasetti 1976). But still – who does not know it? – violence is an endemic human problem. In writing about religion and violence, how can one overlook the continuities of old mentalities in great religious transformations? Or the reality that enforced external takeover and modern social change aggravate violence in reaction, and huge disparities of technical power induce the choler of despair? As adaptations to state control and modernization have been taking place, of course, sublimations of directly harmful violence can see a redirecting of aggressive energies into useful rivalries (in sport and cultural competitions, regional and party-political contending), but they often need serious policing. If no ecumenical steps are taken, confessional or denominational differences can also vitiate ideals of a higher religious unity that was meant to transcend massive tribal divisiveness; and keeping the lid on old physical clashes can drive traditional enmities underground to resurface through increases in sorcery (Trompf 2008a: 291–304, 334–74). In any case, the possibility of engaging in 'modernized military activity' has recurrently appealed, and in liberation movements and civil war we find old and new religious impulses combining to legitimize force.

From the middle of the sixteenth century an increasing minority of Pacific peoples came under different pressures entailed by Western exploration, with the steady opening up of new trade routes across from the Americas to the South East and East Asian islands and eventually to sea-bound Australia. In chronological order, impacts were felt in Micronesia (especially the Marianas, a Spanish colony by 1667), then central Polynesia (especially Tahiti, affected by James Cook's British expeditions (1767–77) and the mutineers of the HMS *Bounty* (1788–90)), and by 1825 in eastern Melanesia; there, sandalwood traders brought disease and deforestation, before 'blackbirding' and 'slaving' started in the 1860s (that is, the recruiting of native people for labour by means of force or deception, mainly Melanesians being cajoled to work on the Queensland cane fields) (esp. Beaglehole 1966). The large island of New Guinea was ostensibly the world's 'Last Unknown' (Souter 1963), considering great populous valleys in its highlands were not accessible to the outside world until the 1930s, with a few secluded pockets still untouched today.

Certainly, by the nineteenth century most of the Pacific had suffered very serious consequences from the unstoppable impact of the outside world: access to firearms and new technologies, depopulation from exposure to foreign diseases, colonial annexations, labour traffic and monetization, as well as expectations that villages alter their production modes. After 1900 came the effects of colonial/imperial control, capital investment (in plantations and mines), world war, postwar modernization and, in some important instances, such as Jayapura, Port Moresby, Nouméa, Honolulu, Wellington, Auckland and other New Zealand cities, intense urbanization and multicultural immigration (numbers of Indian labourers imported to

Fiji rising sharply, for example, and Chinese shopkeepers being successful across Oceania). The religious world of the Pacific, old traditions and converting groups combined, had to confront *Realpolitik* and secularization more abruptly than on Old World continents, and we need to ask sociological questions about the effects of modern 'worldliness' and political realism on contemporary Islander mentalities (Trompf 2004: 241–59) and about whether religion became less a motivator of violence than it had been as a result of these changes. The inflated virtue of bravery in arms, traditionally endemic to Oceania, did not remove itself from group memory overnight, and we know 'mythic consciousness' that glorifies strength can surge back even in a non-theistic ethos, particularly in the name of a new nation's security (Schmitz 1960: 235; cf. Blumenthal et al. 1975: 195–232), and it is a vital part of the Pacific story that Islanders have achieved autonomous control over military instruments of violence at a national level.

A steadying influence throughout modern Pacific history and in social patterns has been the Christian religion, even if through many different churches and at varying levels of comprehension, and this Element will have to account for the confusion, complexities and strains of religious adjustment that have entailed violent outbursts. There were pockets of resistance against colonially associated missionization (as evinced by such new religious movements as 'cargo cults'), and in different strategic ways the Islanders held fast to long-inured local resources to offset the massive disruptions to their spiritual heritage (Campbell 1989; Denoon et al. 2004: 119–323). Oceania's story, of course, is not mainly about negative reactivities. Apart from the remarkable acceptance of Christianity (esp. Forman 1982; Kruczek 2011), Pacific Island countries form a notable bloc among the United Nations. Most attainments of independent sovereignty came after World War II (five in Polynesia, four for Micronesia and at the moment four in Melanesia), with two other polities being member states of New Zealand and participating in UN agencies, and Bougainville now anticipating Independence Day. Eleven entities, however, are dependencies or colonies, and though New Caledonia recently voted to remain a *département* of France, West Papua (made up of the two sizeable Indonesian provinces of Papua and West Papua in easternmost

Indonesia) has only limited autonomy (e.g., Aldrich and Connell 1998: 55–9, 131–6; Firth 2006; and see Fig. 1). All these political rearrangements were accompanied by the growth of churches and local and national Christian leadership, engendering the sense of the Pacific as a sea of Christian countries.

Whatever the varied circumstances, the myriad cultural-linguistic complexes of Oceania, all still reflecting the endogenous religions in their mysterious inheritances, have undergone a mammoth change, and not without tense struggles and expected violence. We have already written about the conundrum of indigenous peoples' willing appropriation of Christian teaching, in spite of the accused complicity of 'Christianity' – nowadays frequently reified as an entity of violence – in European worldwide conquest; but this paradoxical choice revealed to their overlords the savageries they could not see in themselves (Trompf 2007; 2008b), and by concentrating on Islander behaviour we do not want this book to soft-pedal any of the forms of violence inflicted from the outside. It is tempting, of course, to accept a widespread stereotype that Pacific peoples were dragooned into submission or out-wondered by modern technology, or that missionaries duped 'natives' into 'ventriloquising' them and were coercive 'harbingers . . . of a moral economy' called 'capitalism' (V. Smith 1998: esp. 83, 90–2, 128–32; cf. Stipe et al. 1980). Although one can find useful theories of domination and pastoral power (Foucault 1980: 59), conceding also that indigenes' strange-looking experimentations and 'mimicry' might suggest their vulnerability, we would do sad injustice to proud peoples by effacing their power of agency and discrimination. Various missionaries may still send facile reports home of the Gospel's miraculously 'passive recipients', but by more careful documenting we find changes of belief were typically 'discussed and debated', albeit when pressures to convert, given inclinations among neighbouring tribes, were mounting (Neilson 2021: 320). A stress on 'acquiescence' might go some way to explaining a veritable social revolution – the depletion of tribal warfare – which signals a Christianizing Pacific, but why deduce from this a huge inauthentic cave-in or a slavish morality, when in fact inter-lineage decisions about the future involved resolute action and 'the will to change', or not (Fischer 2013: 174–274)? In the end, who did most of the implanting of Pacific churches if it was not the Islanders themselves?

Religious confusion and stress certainly pertained – 'split-level', 'syncretistic' and 'dividualized' behaviour patterns (Schiefenhövel 2009), with 'moral torment' (Robbins 2004) – yet working through intercultural tensions and power-structural hypocrisies has inspired in the Islands welcome new species of personal and social integration (Barker 2019). To try effacing all this, contentious as missionization has been, would be academically irresponsible (Douglas 2001) and nowadays likely to produce a native convert's disgust towards rude innuendos (V. Smith 1998: 12).

On reflection, in writing a book about religion and violence in the post-contact Pacific, one runs the danger of warping history by isolating behaviour that belies both the continuance of traditional conflict-avoiding practices (e.g., Petersen 2014) and the enormous post-contact exertions to inhibit group-imbibed violence. Right from the start, potentials for peaceable relations with strangers were there. Famed Leo Tolstoy saw a key pacifist moment for humanity's history in Russian explorer Nikolai Maklouho-Maclay's daringly unarmed walk among the 'most savage' Rai Coast inhabitants of the Madang area (New Guinea) in 1871, they being awestruck at the white 'moon man' (Tolstoy 1885: 260; Webster 1984). Generally, though, diminishments of violence came in a double movement of complementarity and contradiction – by colonially imposed pacification (new services given for co-operation, yet with breaches of peace incurring punitive expeditions, coercive law enforcement and gaoling) and by propagating the new divine law (obeying the commands 'thou shalt not kill', 'love your enemies', etc. betokening security in God's kingdom, and disobedience alienation from it). A coalescing of these methods might be found in agreements by Church and State that colonial offices ensure native peoples be 'protected, civilized and Christianized' (quoting the Anglican Melanesian Mission's founder-bishop Selwyn (1893–4), upon Britain's appropriation of the southern Solomon Islands), and certainly in-principle rulings and public excoriations against rape, cruelty, sodomy, infanticide and so on by any persons living under Western laws slowly affected even the most isolated rural courts (e.g., Inglis 1974; Stewart 2008). But on the ground there were many tensions over differences of approach, especially between the missionary's protection of the flock and the urgings of officers or businessmen that economic results be hastened.

One should not exaggerate the aspect of progress. Right from the start, admittedly, a spirit of hope for social betterment including 'civilization') pervades the language of missionaries and administrators (not excluding entrepreneurs out to make a quick profit). As the pro-imperial Australian explorer-geographer James Thomson paternalistically reported (1892: 41), after punitive 'social adjustments' on Tubetube and Glenton Island and in other east Papuan contexts, these 'people ... had long earned for themselves a notorious reputation for crimes of murder and rapacity' – at that time against traders, not just enemy tribes – but government actions would hopefully have reduced the number of such obliquities, which had been a 'frequent occurrence in the past'. He was more pessimistic about other places nearer the colonial settlement at Port Moresby, worrying that 'vices previously unknown and inimical to life' (meaning alcohol, tobacco and womanizing), introduced by 'unscrupulous Europeans', might not be easily forestalled by the London Missionary Society (LMS), because a 'demoralising native priesthood' (meaning sorcerers) could appropriate new ways to bolster negative energy against foreign settlers (54–5). In the long run, and overall in the Pacific, though, pressures and instruments to check violent behaviour became cemented as the means to greater social security.

For Australian soldiers and then journalists following the campaign against the Japanese on the north coast of Papua (1942), the fierce Melanesians were completely re-imaged in Western newspapers as crinkly haired carers or 'fuzzy-wuzzy angels' bearing the wounded to safety along the Kokoda Track (Wilson 2016). Instead of warrior chants, today Pacific choristers sing peaceful sacred songs and tour the world, and the Māori *haka* is used as therapy. Even by the end of the Victorian era, 'young people' in central Polynesia were reputedly 'better acquainted with the Bible than the average Sunday School scholars in England' (King 1899: 109), and nowadays the region exports arresting postcolonial theologies (e.g., Havea 2017; cf. Tomlinson 2020). The turbulent highlands of Papua New Guinea (PNG), beginning to be opened up in 1927, became the scene of intense (and ongoing) efforts at intertribal concord, the most durable results coming about through the efforts of longer-serving missionaries (e.g., Strathern and Stewart 2007). For the country's present collective conscience it seems neatly encapsulated by the National Day of Repentance, 26 August 2011.[1] This marked the four-hundredth anniversary of the early Spanish massacre of highly excited and armed (coastal Papuan) Mailu villagers by sailors under the explorer Luis de Torres, including the kidnapping of fourteen children, while inter alia acknowledging that Mailu headhunting raids into the hinterland came to an end in the 1890s through co-operation between the LMS and colonial government.

The shifts and counter-balances of religious valences and conflict have been uncannily multiform in the last few centuries in the Pacific, particularly in Melanesia, and I believe – all too anxiously about my own efforts here – that no learned study can do justice to the intricacies involved. Indeed, when 6 colonies were confederating into the modern nation of Australia (1901), there would still have been over 1,000 tribal wars being waged in the colonies 'next door', where most Islander inhabitants were living locked away. The Second Industrial Revolution had manifested. In 1901, when German steamships could enter Rabaul Harbour (Neupommern/New Britain), their hulls reinforced against bombardment with nickel from the mines of France's New Caledonia (Black 2015; Firth 1983: 115), Europeans who approached the highest reaches of military technology were encountering New Guineans who were still slicing bone arrowheads. The whole enormous surprise already had apocalypse-like proportions (Trompf 1979: 135–6). Then, decades later, came 'messengers from space' – aircraft – and from Pearl Harbor in Hawai'i to Port Moresby, invaders' bombs would also dramatically fall, with traumas of alien intruders, sometimes perceived as arriving in the form of UFOs, eventually showing in scattered psychiatric disorders (Gaisseau 1961; Trompf 1985). How relatively ineffective and utterly marginal the expressions of Pacific Islander violence might seem to be among global belligerencies; yet in its religious worlds, it holds telling, indeed extraordinary stories.

[1] First mooted by a group of churches with Samuel Abal, acting prime minister (incidentally the author's former student), and ratified by his successor as prime minister, Peter O'Neill, in 2011. Cf. *Papua New Guinea Post-Courier*, 30 Aug. 2011.

2 Forms of Religious or Religion-Related Violence in Modern Pacific History and Affairs

It is the purpose of this Element to survey and analyse expressions of religious violence (typically violence bolstered by religious outlooks, sometimes religious agitations leading to violence) within post-contact Pacific Islander life. Adopting a diachronic approach in our overview of the last four centuries, materials from all three great Pacific Island regions are largely handled together, and in rough historical order can be tabulated thus:

- Violent actions and raids against foreigners in early contact situations, often motivated by traditional ways or defence of them, especially in instances when missionaries were killed, but also when Islanders were seized by a desire for new goods, when foreign vessels were at harbour, for example, or made vulnerable.
- Violence inspired by the creation of new religious movements, which often adapted features of the newly introduced religion(s) to the old, with their excitations sometimes generating violent actions of reprisal, even war, against detractors and opponents.
- Collective protests that spilled over into insurrections, rebellions and even war.
- Continuance, yet transformation, of traditional recourses to negative payback.

2.1 Violence against Foreigners

The religious history of the Pacific is strongly memorialized by places where noteworthy foreigners have been felled by the natives. In the earlier-contacted wider Pacific, most of the victims honoured were missionaries and most Catholics – from Jesuit martyr Luis de San Vitores and his catechist, killed in 1672 for baptizing a sick child on Guam against the inviolable order of its father (García (1683) 2004: 251–80), through to Marist (St) Pierre Chanel, clubbed to death in 1841 for allegedly undermining the king of Futuna's sacred authority (Garrett 1982: 97–9). In Melanesia, LMS missionaries John Williams and James Harris, who had

Figure 2 George Baxter's painting *Massacre of the Lamented Missionary the Rev. Williams and Mr Harris, 1841* (National Library of New Zealand, B-088–002)

both become well accepted in central Polynesia, were both slaughtered and eaten by a mass of warriors in 1839 on Erromango (New Hebrides, Fig. 2), as payback for the violence of sandalwood traders against a people already notorious for their cannibal raids (Fakamuria et al. 1995: 395). Wesleyan Thomas Baker and seven Fijian helpers were killed and eaten in 1867 for riskily trying to convert a chief in Viti Levu's mountains (Ryle 2010: 67–9); while Anglican bishop John Coleridge Patteson lost his life at Nukapu (Solomon Islands) in 1871, for being sadly associated with whites stealing young people and with the 'loss' of youths to boarding school (Kolshus and Hovdhaugen 2010).

Over the period from Easter Sunday 1901, when LMS pioneer to Papua James Chalmers and his companions inadvisedly entered a Kerewo long-house on Goaribari Island (off south-west Papua), only to be killed and eaten (Maiden 2003: 97–207), down to the postwar attacks in highland West Papua, especially by the Paniai (1956–7, 1967–70) and Yali groups (1968, 1971)

(Rijksen 1973: 101, 108; Giay 1989: 135–8; Newell 1992: 63; cf. Neilson 2021: 149–216), missionary killing slowly petered out in the later-contacted Melanesian areas. Even as Baker and his fellows fell, so Fijian church lore has it, 'heathenism [was] making its last blind stand', and the son of man making 'the first fatal blow ... became a Christian' next Sunday morning. When Patteson was taken away by two chiefs and slaughtered, arrows were also shot to the man wards his waiting boat with words of payback: 'this for the Bauro man! this the New Zealand man! the Mota man!'[2] The bishop's fate was linked in the press to 'unscrupulous blackbirding'; the killing of natives who had tried to stop their fellows being forcibly recruited had left 'an unforgettable score' that had 'to be settled when opportunity offered' (Bryant 1925: 78–82). When it became obvious the missionaries were very different from the blackbirders, it was soon seen as dishonourable to do them violence, and the difference between martyrdom and group-justified payback killing caught on.

Missionaries generally went unarmed, yet other outsiders with readier recourse to self-defence met sorry fates at the hands of unwelcoming Islanders. Apart from the Hawaiians taking the renowned James Cook, already discussed in the author's prior Element, *Violence in Pacific Islander Traditional Religions* (Trompf 2021a: 59–75)), note how Māori despatched and ate French expeditioner Marion du Fresne and twenty-six members of his crew in the Bay of Islands in 1772, apparently for breaking *tapu* (fishing near the place where bones of the dead were scraped before being laid to rest), but also for their muskets and goods (King 2003: 110, 113). In 1806, nearly all on board the 'pirate treasure ship' *Port-au-Prince* were killed by plundering Tongans off their so-called 'Friendly Islands', nine years after the disastrous LMS attempt to secure a toehold there, with three missionaries being murdered and the survivors eventually escaping to New South Wales in a passing ship (Mariner (1817) 1991: vol. 1, 51–78; 110; Swain and Trompf 1995: 167). Nearly fifty years later the Yâlayu (Balad, northern

---

[2] Naming Bauro (San Cristoval group, Solomon Islands), and Mota (northern New Hebrides/Vanuatu) indicated how widely sourced were islanders willing to recruit with the whites. On Aotearoan involvement, Hamilton 2016.

New Caledonia) massacred crew members of *L'Alcmene* (Bérard [1854] 1978).

In those earlier days, if there was going to be a shift in the perception of Islanders from one defined by the notoriety of their outrages, it could only come about by their participation in European-style maritime business. In the Rewa region of south-eastern Viti Levu, Fiji, where during the 1860s the dominant chief took the Tongan title of Tu'i Kaba, an incoming strategy at that time was to prefer profit from trade over getting a reputation for plunder (Scarr 1976: 98). However, despite taking this cue from the outsiders some Islanders would abet the blackbirding trade in return for new goods; notorious for this were the Polynesian Rotumans and Ni-Vanuatu Tannese, in schooners plying their trade far from home (Chappell 1997: 93). These mavericks felt less moral pressure and were more affected by squabbles *en voyage* when it came to returning indentured labourers (*kanak*s) to their homelands. Setting returnee labourers ashore in the wrong place could mean they could be killed as strangers or by enemies (Corris 1973: 111–25).

In any case, during later-contact Melanesian history, comparable stories of sudden attack can be told. Examples include the attempts to rid the Fly River of the aggressive Italian explorer Luigi d'Albertis on his second (1877) voyage; the effective spearing by (eastern Papuan) Jeannet Islanders of Captain J. C. Craig and the crew on his pearl-diving schooner in 1886; the attacks on Australian miners in mountainous Papua in the 1890s, and on German planters taking land in New Britain (ten unarmed Catholic missionaries easily felled just by association with such theft in 1904); the massacre of the Greig family by Epiritu Santo uplanders (New Hebrides), a people who had a strong tradition of removing strangers (1908); more revenge actions on blackbirders in the Solomons; and, in the case of massacred colonial officer William Robert Bell and his tax-collecting party (in 1927), the removal of the officials who thwarted contact-resistant Kwaio warriors (inland Malaita) from earning bounty for hunting down unavenged enemies (after years of British attempts to stamp out tribal conflict) (Trompf 2008a: 163–5, see also Waiko 1970; Mayo 1973; Keesing 1995). All such onslaughts had their reasons: yes, traditionally strangers, even castaway survivors, were considered spiritually dangerous, but other triggers were more patently connected to religious presuppositions, and with newcomers' flouting and interfering with custom, displaying aggression and withholding marvellous new goods.

In perspective, such violent episodes reflected the teething problems of social change. Under the 'white man's rules', such reactions were instances of murder, not justifiable revenge, and punitive expeditions would show off the whites' superior weaponry; they sometimes fired cannons from formidable naval vessels, presumptively acting out the role of the supra-tribal military guardian. Apart from the curbing effects of such secular and imperial affairs, and the different degrees to which European forces protected missions or not, there came new social demands intersecting with the 'civilizing' of society to meet higher-cultural mores and obey biblical commandments that averted damnation. Not only was peaceable life a high priority for missions; also, idols were to be overthrown, the cooking of human flesh prohibited and orgiastic rites ceased. In Micronesia's Palau, when the zealous Spanish Capuchin Antonio Valencia and his fellows had to pass the figures of fertility goddess Latmîkaik with her gaping vulva that was displayed on clubhouse portals, and that signalled the cult prostitution within, he only reacted by uttering discouraging words about the evils of *lascivia* (lust), and expected all decent persons to agree (Valencia 1891: 12–17; cf. Schlesier 1953: 31–120). Occasions of free association of the sexes on beaches, for which such Central Pacific islands as Tahiti and Rotuma became fabled, were discountenanced by the colonists as unsuitable not only to the holy life but ordinary civic standards as well (e.g., Tanu 1977: 17).

Synoptically, we can gauge that missionary discipline, including the penalties for breaching Church laws that were accepted by Church-supporting chiefs, was strongest in Polynesia (cf. Plate 2005: 93). This would explain why the young Charles Darwin, visiting Tahiti in the *Beagle* (1835), relinquished his assumptions about a gloomy people oppressed through missionization, so well ordered and peaceful was the village life around the simple churches, and so rational and moderate the decision-making in the chiefs' parliament at Matavai Bay (Fitzroy and Darwin 1839), with not a single 'infant-assassin' in sight on islands that had been used to the extensive practice of infanticide before the reforming Pōmare II (Hiney

2000: 55–6; Gunson 1969). Of course religious change brought significant benefits, especially in its lessening of the oppressive manipulation of women and commoners. It did make a social difference that all Tongans had equal access to heaven: non-nobles no longer had to look forward to an afterlife reincarnated as mere vermin! (Latukefu 1974: 8). And when Hawai'i's Queen Kaahumanu, 300-kg beauty and renowned surfer, initiated pro-Christian reforms in 1819, her first move was to break old *kapu*s preventing women and commoners from eating with nobles, before instigating a violent rampage on effigies and temples in sacred places where women had no place. Significantly, accompanying Kaahumanu in this campaign was the visiting Ra'iatean/Tahitian priest-chief and LMS evange-list Auna (Ellis (1842) 1969: 33–54; cf. Maude 1973). Tahiti, then Samoa and Rarotonga, and thereafter Tonga, were to become early leading power-houses of Islander missionary work. Encouraged to look westward, theo-logically trained Polynesian pastors served at south-west Pacific frontiers from 1839 on, Fijians making up the first Melanesian cohorts and with not a few Islander proselytizers being killed for their daring (Crocombe and Crocombe 1994: cf. Brown 1908: 299–322).

The revolutionary shift brought by missionaries, of course, was meant to be quite dissociated from violence. By a certain inevitability, perhaps, mission causes would be temporarily caught up in local wars; some evan-gelizers (like the LMS Polynesian pastors sent along the Papuan coast) felt too nervous to go out without carrying a rifle for warning off would-be attackers (Lovett 1914: 296–7), and others, such as the Marists on the main island (Grande Terre) of New Caledonia (in 1853) had to avoid seeming to be connected to the French warships that were guarding a penal colony too near their footholds (Dousset-Leenhardt 1978: 50–60). And much embar-rassment and pressure for apologetics arose if a mission was accused of abetting violence – as harbour life on Tanna had already been disturbed by blackbirding and intertribal strife (Paton 1889; 100–22; Adams 1984: 168–81). On Tuvalu, the promise of 'new beginnings' is now mainly associated with the coming of the LMS (whose members had arrived from the south by 1862), but also with the setbacks of problematic violence: the islet of Te Afua Fou had its name tweaked to reflect the old order/tide rushing out for a new one at the time when a native was gunned down for stealing from a white navigator; while on far-north Niutao, the last place to convert, a stubborn chief who had vehemently refused to follow the others in doing so was speared to death (Munro 1982: 80–134; Hedley 1896: 17). Generally, however, despite constant setbacks and disputes between denominational flocks (Trompf 2008a: 291–304), apostolic pacifism lit the beacon for the future socio-religious and political management of 'the Christian Pacific'. Countless individual moralities were altered (Barker 2016, Hemer 2013: 147–74), ecclesial regulations (including Canon Law) were applied (e.g., Sarei 1974) and government judicial appointees had to work out Western penalty systems appropriate to highly unusual contexts (as we see from the example of the Germans in the Pacific, who meticulously fine-tuned their ordinances and consistently followed them (Sack 2001: 405–601)). In the discordances of the colonial ethos and the violence that was expected to arise as part of that system, baptized native police would be deployed to suppress, even execute, lawbreakers and rebels (Kituai 1998: 42–137). Indeed, as subalterns ordered to fight, the distinctively black Buka Islanders were sent as soldiers to put down the 1904 Maji Maji Rebellion in Germany's far-off Tanganyika (Sayers 1930: 30). Half a century later, as one aged Saibai Island veteran recently reminisced, when the Japanese bombed the Torres Strait (1942), a light infantry battalion was required, 'to keep Australia free ... Aborigines, Europeans, Islander boys – we broke bread with everyone, we're brothers' (*Sydney Morning Herald* (= *SMH*) 12 Jun. 2021: 20). By the turn of the millennium, and in spite of its internal turmoils, Fiji could claim the worthiest record of international military service among independent Pacific nations, even sending UN peacekeepers to the Holy Land (*Fiji Today* 2003: 18–19).

As religious change progressed, expectedly, the development of Pacific missionization and emergent Islander Christianity took on increasing complexity, as denominational zones of operation were established. There was also an extraordinary multiplication of mission stations, churches, evangelizing organizations and Bible translation projects, especially due to the involvement of new foreign personnel – in PNG, the most noticeable of these groups were Americans in the period after World War II, Catholic Poles free to leave post-Cold War Europe in the 1990s, and recently South Asians (Trompf and Tomasetti

2023). From a distance, it seems a real flurry. Other-than-Christian religions, such as the Baha'i faith and Islam, enter more strongly in recent times into this busy hive. There was violence of every kind somewhere in the histories of religious change in the Pacific; if there were only very rare shootings by Christian missionaries in self-defence (e.g., Flichler et al. 1938: 7, 14), jealousy over access to missions could worsen old tribal animosities (e.g., Hogbin 1970: 135). Insensitvity toward 'heathen ways' brought destruction and appropriation of objects (King 2011) (native evangelists often showing great enthusiasm; Schieffelin 1981), with disproportionately cheap acquiring of land and discourse of 'conquest' for the Gospel (often in the context of 'inter-sectarian strife' (Trompf 2008a: 291–304); the latter led to occasions when indigenous mission personnel were sent to drive out evangelizing intruders on their patches and burn their properties (e.g., *NGAR* (*New Guinea Annual Report*) 1935: 25–9)).

In mission life, corporal punishment by schoolteachers was typically the norm (and is holding on even now, despite formal acceptance of internation-ally encouraged prohibitions (e.g., McLean 2014)). In frontier contexts, mind you, one would expect active indigenous supporters of 'the mission' to plead the 'cause for no beating of the boys and no ordeals or "initiation" rites' (Gajdusek 1967: 131), and if in the past near-pubescent boys faced initiatory circumcision, the Abrahamic connections of this practice did not prevent it from dwindling: even on Takaroa (French Polynesia), where Mormon converts had been convinced they were the descendants of the lost Israelites, by the early twentieth century 'the kids' had gained the right to say they 'don't appreciate it' (O'Brien 1922: 111). For arrant misbehaviour, of course, evangelists or teachers faced 'suspension' (e.g., Gunn and Gunn 1924: 129–30); though if instruction involved carelessly misquoting the Bible, only shaming applied, as the traditional penalties of death for wrongly reciting prayers and chants (in Polynesia, Mülhmann 1955: 22) were now considered abhorrent. Still, species of institutional bullying have to be reckoned with, along with the phenomenon of some ministers lording over infant congrega-tions, with Polynesian pastors too commonly domineering over Melanesian 'blacks' (e.g., Eri 1973: 7). Other problems were that Europeans ordered much work to be done without their own personal involvement, and protected their own space for fear their lives would become unbearable, with too many muddy visitors (compare Mantovani 2021: 26–44). 'Patri-kyriarchal' attitudes in the Church, their background in both Pacific traditional realities and Western male chauvinism, inevitably let in forms of violence against women's vulnerabilities (Filemoni-Tofaeono and Johnson 2006). These are all issues missions now have to recognize, own and address responsibly in works to repair 'lasting damage' (Gesch 2009; May 2003: esp. 32–49, 57–60).

In a realistic perspective, though, we can see that Pacific Islander violence in reaction to missions and mission personnel progressively diminished to a virtual nil, in spite of such imperfections. This was in large part because the churches were the grounding and stable structures in Pacific life as millions of villagers entered the modern world, with communal gatherings, schools, workshops, clinics and projects (including road-building) sustaining most of the burden of social development in the post-contact histories of so many isolated and 'globally marginal' places. The churches survived and cushioned the Islands through international conflict, and in moments of serious political hiatus, as between the withdrawal of the Dutch and stronger Indonesian engagement in Irian Jaya/West Papua (esp. 1961– 5), or through civil war (in the Solomons, 1998–2003) – for two glaring examples – they were almost the only institutions supplying daily infrastructure and allowing life to go on 'undramatically' in rural areas (Neilson 2021: 239–69; Hviding 2011: 52).

But by far the most important factor in the Christian success story pertains to the forgotten sociology of attitudes, especially in significantly raised levels of trust among peoples very suspicious of each other. As distinct from other introduced fixtures (government, business, most higher education bodies and non-profit organizations, or NGOs), the churches' ideals of love and goodwill, peace, justice, truth and behaviour were presented as *sacred*, and sacrality was already fundamental to holding together endogenous human groupings. As one Massim informant long ago assessed the situation, before contact there was only 'respect' for one's people and 'our own dead': the enemy was just a 'thing' (*gogo*) and a captive 'our meat' (*gum*; payback flesh); and neither was thought of as 'a person' – certainly not part of a wider community of sacred persons (Macintyre 1995:

35). Colonial officials were always the potential agents of coercive control, and had to be alert for the 'build up' of 'civil disturbances' and to assess whether 'extreme force should be used' (Ryan 1973: File 58–18–1), and governments have exerted such prerogatives for themselves to sponsor excessive mining and even use islands as atomic testing sites – in the case of Micronesia's Marshalls, with shocking irresponsibility. The churches, with their special 'contrariness', stood 'in the way' of martial impersonalism, ruthlessness and de-spiritualizing energies (Burridge 1991: esp. 35–70). Uneven though the Islands' imbibing of new values has been and still is across an enormous arena (Robin 1980: 275–6), and complicit as Church infrastructure inevitably has been in the emergence of political and resource frontiers (e.g. Gascoigne 2014; Jacka 2015), evangelized Christian principles provided the means to adjudge hypocrisy both within and outside the Church, make comparisons with the forces of 'this world' and cultivate a hope of being 'made free' as humans and even of securing Exodus-like liberation from oppression.[3] This stirred the 'spirit of independence' that would indigenize churches and ensure they outlasted decolonization or regime change (cf. Maxwell 2005) and energize new social movements and reformist projects, including independent churches and the adopting of spiritistic/Pentecostal worship as a revolution of religious autonomies in rupture from missions bound by European forms. Yet, however much Christian teaching affected them, not all of these movements eschewed violence, and we will have to attend to a variety of those that did not in some detail.

2.2 New Religious Movements of Resistance

Especially during the late nineteenth into the twentieth centuries, European imperializing powers established control over the Pacific Islands. These powers consisted of: Spain (in Micronesia from 1565–1898); France (in Tahiti and French Polynesia from 1842, Nouvelle-Calédonie, 1853,

---

[3]　Using John 18:36, 8:32 and Exod. 7–14. In Christian thought, the Exodus is honoured because the oppressed Jewish slaves relied on God unarmed; in contrast, note that armed rebellion, even in the Old Testament, is depreciated: for example, 2 Sam. 13–19; I Kings 12.

Nouvelles-Hébrides (with Great Britain), 1906 etc.); Great Britain (in New Zealand from 1840, Fiji, 1874, British New Guinea, 1888, Gilbert and Ellice Islands (now Kiribati and Tuvalu), 1892, Solomons, 1893 etc.); the Netherlands (Nieuw Guinea, from 1872); Germany (in the period leading up to at least 1914, in Neuguinea from 1885, German Micronesia, 1890, Samoa, 1900 etc.); Chile (Rapanui, from 1888); United States of America (Guam, 1898, Hawai'i, 1898 etc.); Australia (Papua, first in 1883–7 and then from 1902 onwards, and New Guinea, 1914); New Zealand (the Cooks, from 1901, Samoa, 1914, etc.); Japan (Palau, etc. from 1914); Indonesia (in West Papua, from 1963). The capacity of these powers to send out expatriate personnel and organize modern industries and the labourizing of indigenes was immense, and it was especially irksome to locals that although the outsiders had no 'traditional suzerainty' over them (Ratuva 2013: 12) they could behave arrogantly and arbitrarily towards potential 'cannibals' (Denoon et al. 2004; cf. Thomas 1990; Quanchi and Adams 1993: 31–112).

By and large, superior firepower meant that local people's physical resistance to foreign domination, in all reality, was usually fruitless, and at any rate the overall effect of evangelization meant the disappearance of tribal war coincided with rise of colonial law, a territorially wider social order and emergent socio-economic opportunities. The development of missionary spheres makes up a complex story, with the Catholics being found in most of Micronesia (from 1668) and many places throughout Oceania; the combined-Protestant LMS (from 1796) in Tahiti, Samoa, the Cooks, the Gilbert and Ellice Islands and south-coast Papua; Anglicans and the Church Missionary Society (or CMS; from 1814) especially in New Zealand, Hawai'i, the New Hebrides, the eastern Solomon Islands and northern Papua; the Protestant American Mission Board (ABCFM; from 1820) on Hawai'i and in Micronesia; Wesleyans or Methodists (from 1822) mostly in Tonga, Samoa, New Zealand, Fiji, New Guinea Islands, south-eastern and island Papua, and the western Solomons; the Church of Latter-day Saints (from 1844) in the Tuamotus and wider Polynesia; the Dutch Reformed (from 1855) in Nieuw Guinea; the Reformed Presbyterians in the New Hebrides (from 1858); the Lutherans (from 1866) in Deutsch-Neuguinea and the wider Pacific; and others such as the Queensland Kanaka Mission, the Seventh-Day Adventists (SDAs), the Churches of

Christ in Australia and the Unevangelized Fields Mission (UFM), as well as many more smaller affairs, coming later. This is not to forget the marginal effects of Islam (first in Raja Ampat Islands, West Papua, from *c*.1500); Shinto and Buddhism (northern Marianas 1919); Baha'ism (Gilberts, 1954), and many others that formed parts of the whole picture (Forman 1992; Trompf 2004: 141–87; with Ramsted 2003: 66–9; Neilson 2021: 4; Astroth 2019: 44–6; Hassell 2005). Local peoples' vital involvement in proselytizing needs recognition, including its role in the development of 'national' and decolonized denominations and the rise of independent churches (similar to those in southern Africa and the US South; Trompf 2018).

Generally, the history of violence in religious resistance movements from immediate precolonial contexts to the larger religio-political context of 'contemporary history' was a muted one. Collective actions more often took the form of non-cooperation, if often in highly unusual forms, which had the capacity to spill over into the use of physical force. There were, of course, conflicts right in the interface between tradition and the new order which had to work themselves out. In the dying embers of the Tongan empire in the Lau Islands (eastern Fiji), for instance, much to missionaries' despair in the 1850s, vicious skirmishes over inter-island power occurred between Tongan warlords and Fijian chiefdoms that had intermarriage connections with Tonga. A sudden massacre of seventeen leading Christians, including a Fijian chief and his wife, at Lomaloma on Vanua Balavu (in the Lau Islands) in 1853, meant Lau Islander Christians looked to the Tongan prince 'Enele Ma'afu, emergent champion of Methodism (in the region of its Fijian beginnings), to settle matters militarily, which suited his project of unifying an eastern Fijian 'kingdom' (as its *Tu'i Lau*). Now, meanwhile the great Chief Seru Cakobau of Bau (lord of the cannibalistic complex described in our earlier Element: *Violence in Pacific Islander Tranitional Religions*) converted to Christianity and gave up both cannibalism and polygyny, mainly at the urging of Tonga's King George Tupou I (Trompf 2021a: 50–1, 69–70), who promised him a schooner after his showy royal visit to Sydney. The reaction of those benefiting from the old system was decisive; rebels already questioning Cakobau's right of succession and many of his traditional Rewa River enemies consolidated at a key arsenal on the Kaba peninsula, and could not be overcome until all the double-canoes King George could muster came to his aid (Feb. 1855). In what was clearly 'not a typical '"holy war"', there occurred the siege and great Battle of Kaba, 'pivotal' in Fijian history, with 200 killed and many more wounded using European weapons (Grainger 1992: 30–5; Spurway 2015; with Scarr 1976; Garrett 1982: 114).

Cakobau, the man who once affirmed 'it is good for us to war until all our enemies are killed', followed George's lead in being lenient to the rebels, executing no one. Although the Tongans departed (Fijians on both sides feared they might not), and although Cakobau then dominated the rising bêche-de-mer trade and later declared himself 'king' of *all* Fiji, dissident elements on the big island of Viti Levu remained a scourge. Meanwhile Ma'afu's role beside George in the Battle of Kaba strengthened his (Tongan) lordship over the eastern isles, and this determined the west/ east, Melanesian/more Polynesian divide in the struggle for Fiji's future united nationhood (Thornley 2000: 70–81). Trouble in the big island's centre, not contained by Cakobau, was left to the British to resolve (Cakobau and Ma'afu ceded Fiji to them, and it became a Crown Colony in 1874). The colonials handled the 'small war' of 1876 resulting from Chief Nacanikalou (his naming meaning 'God's Curse') defending his people's sacred lands in the hills with some guns, and then the 1885 Tuka movement. The latter movement was sparked by a traditional priest called Navosavakadua ('The One Speaking Once'), who prophesied in the rugged Ra region that a time would come when whites would serve blacks and then set up a spiritually armed military-style order with 'sergeants' and 'soldiers' called 'destroying angels' (Stanmore 1879: vol. 2, 100–1; Sutherland 1908– 10: 56 (quotations); Kaplan 1995: 10–12 and passim).

The faster-firing American Snider rifle made British control in the Pacific easier (from 1853), and was crucial in the outcome of New Zealand's so-called Land Wars (1846–72), which were prolonged by religious energies that opposed the alienation of land from the Māoris that was taking place despite the promising 1835 Declaration of the Independence of New Zealand, signed by fifty-two Northern Island chiefs and the British Resident James Busby. By mid-century, the chiefs had divided over collaboration with the foreigners. Many turned against growing settlement intrusion (mainly in central North Island), at first simply fighting defensively under the protection of a district war deity, Maru, until traditional war councils were re-established (from 1853) and an independent monarchy was proclaimed. Potatau, from the Waikato, became first ruler of the 'King (or *Kīngitanga*) movement' in 1858, as repository of the Māoris' collective *mana*, the inalienable sacrality (*tapu*) of their land and the hope of its potential recovery from theft ('a form of violence', anyway) (see Wilkes 2019: 224–8). Such unprecedented solidarity was to meet the gaping divide between two ways of being (cf. Douglas 1998: esp. 281), the biggest clash territorially and demographically in the Pacific by that time; unifying meant empowerment for successful military victory. In the course of intermittent bouts of conflict, syncretic prophetic teachings percolated. Wesleyan convert Te Ua Haumêne (d. 1866) joined the King movement and served as a chaplain (1860s), until an experience of the archangel Gabriel led him to conceive the Māori as the new Israel. The true Israelites needed to be ready to cast out 'the pale beings' (*pākehā*) or disinherit them from the Holy Land, an outlook conveyed in the sacred scripture *Ua Rongo Pai* ('The Gospel According to Us'), which combined biblical and traditional values and set out the Pai Mārire ('the Good, Peaceable Way') (Sinclair 1961; Cowan 1923: vol. 2, 1–15; Dalton 1967: 207–8; McLaughlin 2017).

Although it was originally detached from warrior activity, violent acts come steadily into the *Pai Mārire* story, perhaps even very early on, if the account of Te Ua symbolically sacrificing his own child is true. The successful Māori surprise attack on the Ahuahu settler village in 1864 gave the King movement conviction that its forces could fight under Gabriel's protection, with Te Ua claiming he could talk to Jehovah through the severed heads of Captain Lloyd and of other soldiers who had been slain with him. But Te Ua also called for trust in the power of a war-cry incantation imparted by Gabriel to cause the bullets of the enemy to fly past without hitting, and in the 1864 assault on the solidly defended and newly threatening Sentry Hill, New Plymouth, thirty-four Māori warriors fell dead because they marched towards enemy rifle fire in faith, with right arms held high, chanting '*Hapa, hapa, hapa! Hau, hau, hau!*' ('go wrong through the air/pass over'). A year later at Opotiki, Bay of Plenty, when Carl Völkner of (the Anglican) Church Missionary Society was hanged from a willow tree by Pai Mārire leaders as an alleged government spy – his own Māori congregation assenting, his head cut off, his blood smeared on his killers' lips and his eyes gouged out and swallowed by ex-Catholic Kereopa Te Rau, one of Te Ua's 'prophets' – it was clear that a radicalizing of land-war ideology had occurred. *Hauhau*, as the dogma and its adherents were known, spread like wildfire, but its fanatical aspects soon brought suppression and select reprisal hangings in 1865 under Governor George Grey and his Māori allies (though para-doxically, Te Ua went free) (Rosenfeld 1999: 107–16; Lyall 1979; Winks 1953).

The Māoris' military skills earned them great respect, their digging of protective ditches and bunkers around their *pâ*s giving them the reputation of having inspired modern trench warfare. Their armed resistance also lasted (in the rugged north-eastern Te Urewera area of North Island) until 1921, when the longest-lasting indigenous reliance on violence for survival against foreign intrusion in the Pacific came to an end (Belich 1982; Binney 2019). Both Te Urewera and King Country (the domain claimed by the Māori kings after Potatau, on the opposite side of the North Island) gave sanctuary to the renowned raiding force under Te Kooti Arikirangi (d. 1893), who legitimated his 'guerilla attacks' as the removal of Amalekites (the whites) by the true inheritors of Israel (the Māori) (see 1 Sam. 15:3). During earlier fighting on the government's side against *hauhau*, Te Kooti had been accused of spying (by pro-government Māori) and exiled without trial to the Chatham Islands; however, he escaped with 168 prisoners, using a captured schooner and his youthful experience as a seaman. The successful crossing back to the North Island was likened to the Israelites' Exodus from Egypt, though it involved sacrificing Te Kooti's uncle (by throwing him overboard) when the ship was temporarily becalmed. The movement's 1868 slaughter of fifty-four Matawhero townspeople, including women and children and twenty-two Māori (apparently to avenge the false allegations of spying), brought on the so-named Te Kooti War (1869–72) and the exertions of British punitive power. Te Kooti escaped again, and in King Country had time (especially once he had been officially pardoned) to elaborate the redeemer religion of Ringatū that he had founded in writing (Misur 1973; Rosenfeld 1999: 191–202; cf. Binney 1984: 351–8; Greenwood 1980).

In prophesying Māori recovery, we see Te Ua and Te Kooti as precursory figures of prophet-led movements that preserved indigenous identity by appealing to Old Testament motifs of overcoming slavery, exile and suffering. Ringatū, which emerged in the 1880s as the first in a cluster of Māori independent churches, provides a useful clue to the lasting spiritual energies that brought hope of liberation to the Māori into the twentieth century and beyond, though without violent agendas (Elsemore 1985; Webster 1979; Binney et al. 1979; Mikaere 1997). To confirm our earlier framing, moreover, the cosmological assumptions are indicatively vertical, looking upwards for power. In Te Ua's conception, those getting killed in his cause 'would be glorified' and 'stand on the roof of clouds'; for Te Kooti's Ringatū, the eagle is the major symbol of God, ready to pounce and also bring Law from above. Later on, the strong separatist church honouring Tahupotiki Ratana's teachings (from 1928) portrays heaven and earth iconically with a ladder reaching up from a car to an aeroplane (Swain and Trompf 1995: 184–5; Clark 1975: 10). Our allusion to the spiritual dimension of new goods will immediately call to the mind a famous feature of adjustment and resistance movements, expectation of 'the cargo'; but before we turn to these ideas as widespread in Melanesia, a few further comments on looking up to heaven and for 'heavenly providing' in Micronesia and Polynesia are called for to help bridge our analyses.

In Tahiti, interestingly, when the so-called Mamaia spirit movement erupted (from 1826) each commoner prophet (*peropheta*) instigating disobedient behaviour claimed they had direct 'access to heaven', usually by Jesus' or God's inspiration (through possession states) to override missionary 'lies'. The new (biblically based) laws of Pōmare II for running the country were rejected and polygyny was restored, amid an abundance of feasting, dancing and 'enjoyments made . . . boundless' in a denial of a 'real' hell. On Maupiti in the Leeward Islands, where this 'heresy' held everyone's attention and its enticements made for good inter-island propaganda, 'a shipload of cloth from the skies' was promised, and Islanders 'made a large boat to bring the ship from above', expecting from it 'swarms of fish . . . wine from heaven in bottles' and 'cows out of the clouds'. Their deviations could incur severe punishments in the name of the Christianizing monarch, such as being made to walk on reefs in bare feet, though these official sanctions brought on threats of violence in return. Mamaia followers exacerbated the internal conflict on the Leewards, but in the fighting 'many of them were slain'; and from Moorea (off Tahiti) 'war was imminent', with insurrectionists supporting Mamaia armed 'with Bayonets, Swords and old Muskets', having been promised victory by prophets (who had traditional roles as 'battle augurs'). In a battle in February 1832, Queen Pōmare IV's forces won after three hours of fighting at Tai'arapu (southeast Tahiti), with around twenty-five rebel heads beaten to pulp (Gunson 1962: 212, 214–15, 217, 221, 223, 226, 228, 232–3, 235–41; with Mühlmann 1955: 213–52). Attempts to restore the old ways slid away thereafter in a Christianizing yet precolonial context, a process sped up by the effects of a smallpox epidemic nine years later (until the French extinguished Mamaia activities altogether, after its leaders refused missionary efforts at vaccination).

A few minor episodes somewhat like this occurred a century after in the wider Pacific. A disturbance on Onotoa in the southern Gilberts (of Micronesia) had one Ten Naewa arising out of the LMS fold to oppose the presence of Catholics on the atoll (1930). First declaring Jesus would soon descend to help his cause, he went one strange step further by self-designating as 'God the Father'. Attracting mostly females, he appointed men as 'Swords of Gabriel' to enforce more male compliance with his teaching, and until British officers stopped his movement in its tracks, his followers, processing after Naewa's contorted dance, had put four Catholics to death (Grimble 1932; 1952: 93–100; Nevermann 1968: 77). Here there is violence but no interest in new goods, while on the Polynesian outlier of Rennell Island in 1938, there was little violence but a desire to replace the influences of three different missions and procure European items, while breaking down old gender taboos. A Rennell prophet and adopted son of a traditional priest, one Tegheta, sent off three messengers 'to heaven' to bring down calico, the supply of which the foreigners controlled; on Rennell and nearby Bellona, great men sought to accost the sky gods for perceived injustice. Tegheta even abrogated tabus against sexual intercourse with his classificatory mother and sister. Group shaking following these surprising developments caused the missionaries to call it all 'madness', and in any case failed outcomes from the gods brought on mass conversion to Christianity (Elbert and Monberg 1965: 401–14; Stewart and Strathern 2018: 6). Such outbursts of novel religious activities in Micronesia and on Polynesian outliers were few and far between, but in Melanesia new religious movements and the emergence black independent churches were notably multifarious.

We can allow that most new religious movements in the south-west Pacific could be fairly dubbed 'cargo cults', that is, they can merit this epithet (but hopefully without disparagement)[4] when villagers were collectively encouraged to await an abundance of European-style trade goods, borne miraculously (or in a manner beyond the ordinary course of things) by their ancestors or culture heroes or deities, even Jesus. Having written extensively on cargo-cult phenomena myself, I should remind readers of a wide range of expectations (from the hoped-for coming of many tins of bully beef to a full cornucopia of valued non-traditional objects, from steel pots to motor vehicles) and a broad spectrum of group efforts (from a minor stir in a village where an isolated upstart announces the 'key to the cargo' (in Pidgin/pidgins, *Kago*) to highly organized networks of villages working to disrupt the normal run of life; Trompf 2011: 438–41; 2020a–b). Why the Black Islands spawned many movements of hope for easy access to these new goods is an important question. After all, all Islanders found in the foreigners' accoutrements objects of wonder. A near-contact conversation with Māori on board a British ship about to arrive in Australia (1828), for instance, led some Māori to believe that the vessel's magnetic binnacle was guided by 'the white man's gods' and that Sydney's windmills were deities and muskets to be 'actually worshipped' (Earle 1832: 276–8). But 'wondering about wonder' like this can become a full-time analytical preoccupation in Melanesian studies because south-west Pacific religiosities are 'all-comprehensive' in that well-being is expressed as much through materiality as it is through health, relationships with humans and spirits, altered states and so on (Lawrence 1954: 10–11; Whiteman 2002: 67; Trompf 2003: 302–9). To pass Melanesian religions off as distinctly 'materialistic', mind you, can miss the point that, in their view, the 'surprise and excess' of fecundity and bounty are expressive of total vitality, or of 'life' as an all-present divinity, and

---

[4] Stigma accruing from their pasts impel some Melanesian groups to debar the phrase 'cargo cult' locally, even punishing those who use it and break this tabu: Hermann 1987.

so the appearance of goods outside the realm of day-to-day experience suddenly added dimensions to the possibilities of being (Mantovani 1977: Gesch 1990). Indeed, since the arrival of European-style goods ended millennia of Stone Age technology, such *Kago* was 'structurally eschatological', marking the momentous change of an old, hard-lived order into an astounding new one (Trompf 2004: 47).

By experience, of course, black people were to learn that dealing with the white people and their possessions typically ended in 'illusory promises of the abundant life'. 'Your countrymen are gods', was a common Fijian exclamation to missionaries, as was 'You are a *kalou* [divine]!', an expression of astonishment at white inventions (Williams 1858: 2016); but soon the Fijian chiefs would have to cede executive powers to the foreigners because the introduction of new technology brought serious disorder from both tribesmen and traders (Macnaught 1982: 12–63). In the Melanesian heartlands, the history of reactions induced collective ritual activity: upon holding metal pots and utensils in the 1870s; seeing the transition from sailing to steamships; the world's first regular freight flights across Papua and New Guinea in the 1930s; the great US aircaft carriers disgorging tanks, amphibians and jeeps at the Momote airbase on Manus during World War II; and on to helicopters bringing missionaries and supplies to remote valleys in the 1950s. Prophetic announcements were made that the Cargo was on its way: attempts at wharf construction occurred along with the clearing of landing places, sometimes with wooden aeroplanes, would-be radios and aerials being made and rituals of preparation performed. In earlier phases of individual movements such anticipations sometimes took on a frenzied aspect, including the destruction of pigs and property out of faith that a dramatic transformation would occur. And if hopes lasted, these rituals changed into more weekly, routinized forms, such as caring for ritual gardens for welcoming back the dead, multiplying financial resources, planning new villages, creating an alternative church, even building facilities to have more babies for a community set apart from any others around (esp. Strelan 1977: 13–50; Trompf 2008a: 194–258).[5]

---

[5] Experiences in the 'white man's world' were the making of 'cult' leaders, who witnessed or worked on the construction of wharves or airstrips (early illustrations of the former are found in Angas 1866: 169; Rosenberg 1878: 441).

Explanatory ideas that intensified hopes for Cargo included the claim that the whites had powers to steal or divert goods which the spirit world really intended for Melanesians; that in the mythic past culture heroes had offered the choice between Cargo and old technics but the people had rejected the former as apparently useless; that Cargo treasure lay hidden inside a mountain or cave waiting to be revealed; that when Cargo arrived blacks would regain their lost prestige or turn into whites; and so on (see Trompf 2008a: 259–81; Turner 1978: 46, 48–9, 52). All this belongs within 'the contact situation' (between 'primitives' and 'moderns') synoptically conceived as 'an integral whole' (Malinowski 1945: 14).

We talk of cargo cults when groups are collectively energized to wait for the imminent arrival of European-style (now internationally marketed) commodities, or containers of money as their equivalent. They could be classed sociologically as a subspecies of 'millenarian movements' (or expressing 'commodity millennialism') (Talmon 1966: 165, 169–70, footnotes; Wilson 1973: 309–47; Landes 2011: 59–69; cf. Trompf 2011: 439–42), yet just expecting the miraculous arrival of tinned meat in plentiful quantities hardly seems a millennium. The millenarian aspect looks obvious, by comparison, in the case of the so-called Kukuaik cult on volcanic Karkar Island (Madang region, 1941–2), which at its height pinned hopes on the Japanese invading to punish the 'arrogant Europeans'. After their actions, all the futurist mission talk that had earlier inspired local yearnings for betterment was to be actualized: Jesus, often blurred with the Islanders' deities and ancestors, would arrive in a ship laden with cargo, signalled by eruptions, the sun's eclipse and other cosmic signs in a mix of Christian and homespun eschatologies (Hannemann 1948: 948–9, with McSwain 1979: 67–8, 73–4, 89–90, 93–7). Then again, there surely has to be a distinctive outburst of *organized* collective preparedness for a 'high transformation' to make a 'cargo cult': otherwise it is just dreaming or a pervasive hope (what we can call 'cargoism') (Trompf 1990: 13–15). And perhaps a concerted imitation and appropriation of white behaviour is just not enough, as with the Polynesian Siovili or 'Joe Gimlet' cult (Samoa, 1827), despite its talk of the next 'man-of-war' bringing 'knives, musket-balls and ramrods', albeit sent by 'the King of the Skies' and meant to clinch an independent life for the Islanders (Freeman 1959: 194–6). We suggest, then, that cargo cultism or cargo movementscan be justly typologized as such for carrying a distinctive phenomenality, and when it comes to generalizing about Melanesia, we should also insist that they are but one kind of 'new religious movement' there and that while some of these can be just plainly millenarian or 'catastrophic', others are more 'nativistic', unacculturated, protestative or very spiritually focused, and not especially focused on *Kago* (Laracy 1983; Loeliger and Trompf 1985: xii–xi; Trompf 2015).

Now, the question arises: are Melanesian cargo cults noted for their violent activity? Not really. If we take the most exhaustive comparative register of their features (by Friedrich Steinbauer in an Erlangen doctoral thesis), just over 10 per cent of the 186 movements he cites set up any kind of military-looking organization; one famous one, honouring the mysterious Jonfrum on Tanna (Vanuatu), has to this day kept up some daily drilling, while about another 10 per cent, in one form or another, created a situation of 'terror', though not necessarily followed by violent actions (Steinbauer 1971: post-495 ff.). Paradoxically, movements fantasizing about drastic change have usually been realistic in the face of irresistible armaments: dreaming of 'world reversal' thus involves more projection and readiness for drastic social change than realization by force, even if mobilization for an expected transformation might bring about enough wriggle room to create satisfying new homegrown institutions (Worsley 1970: 257–60, 263–4, cf. 193–204 with Cohn 1970 for theory and theoretical background). Still, violence has been a component in the cargo-cult story, and, as I have argued elsewhere, cargo dreams create the potential for physical harm against those who question the likelihood of, or oppose their fulfilment (Trompf 2008a: 197–201). If we can generalize cautiously, human groups are known to coagulate around what others will deem an exaggerated expectancy (or 'false rumours' of the future). Once interaction between insider believers and outsiders takes place, with negative responses to apparent 'wrongheadedness' being induced (in the Pacific Islands first by village elders or church leaders), an *altercation* has occurred. The dreamers have been noticed; they have caused a stir; resentful for being rejected, they close ranks, sensing they are 'on to something'. At the least they will not co-operate with scorners or authorities; at the most they will be ready or get worked up enough to fight for their prospectively splendid, cosmic 'place in the sun'. They climb up a magical rope, as the sociologist of hope Henri Desroche has it (1979: 1–4, 69–71), and if circumstances permit the group energy sufficient clout and freedom, it somehow 'holds', generating a distinct socio-religious movement.

Thus see the following figure, Fig. 3.

A spectrum of possibilities presents itself from the data. In a near-contact situation, immediate frustration at the loss of warrior power and economic prestige could express itself in desperate magico-ritual procedures to create the items the white intruders dominated. In 1949, among the Western New Guinea highland Wahgi (whose community was opened to the outside world as late as 1933) the goods most sorely lacking were *kina*-shell money (which carriers bore in abundant boxed supply for white patrol officers), steel axes and guns. Orchestrated by one Goitaiye Dolpe of Mur, committed Kumai tribesmen joined together to construct an enclosed palisade around a traditional dance-ground for fertility and pig-killing ceremonies. They piled vegetables and prepared pigs in a large cult house within, and dancers decorated themselves and bore traditional weapons ready for dancing. Meanwhile

(0.) Mutual co-existence
1. Resentment repressed, yet 'seething under the surface' of local and colonial affairs
2. The creation of an altercation
3. The contentious refusal to co-operate with the masters/setting up of an alternative way
4. Open confrontation with limited violence
5. Violent conflict

Figure 3 A schematized spectrum of reactions to outside interference

Goitaye performed rituals at the edges of an isolated high lake; leaf-parcels scooped from its waters were passed down along a hundred-strong line of hopeful followers to sit eventually in the cult house, ready for transformation into the desired goods as the dancing burst forth. As the day continued, though, no change occurred: nonetheless, Goitaye insisted on prolonging these efforts and warriors from further afield came to join 'the work'. Each day the dancers became more frenetic and by evening time would poke their spears ferociously through the palisade walls at the ever-crowding nervous onlookers. Ritual mock-attacks by hosts against invited guests, known in Wahgi pig-killing festivals, could have turned seriously violent here in bursts of extreme action. The frenzy eventually dissipated, though, and the food needed to be distributed and consumed anyway; but further into Wahgi country, two enterprising souls tried setting up alternative police systems, one clearly for getting 'rid of the Europeans', with guns prophesied to 'shoot the patrol officers, if they dared to interfere' (Trompf 1989a: esp. 266–73, with Reay 1959: 196–7).[6]

Elsewhere we can find cargo activities with instructive similarities and differences. Frenzied dancing (so-named choreomania, Gotman 2018: 261–2) and collective possession or manic behaviour marked the so-named 'Vailala Madness' (1919–22, central Elema, Papuan Gulf), and yet there was little violence except in the rampant destruction of masks and paraphernalia belonging to the traditional cultus, an act of apparent shame (Williams 1923). Enthusiastic ritual dance carried out to turn wooden staves into rifles among the central New Guinea highland Dene (in 1953) seems immediately comparable to the Wahgi scenario (if well east of it), yet without threat to life or limb in what was more an 'early contact cult' (Salisbury 1958). But some episodes brought frenzy and violence together. Captivated by the young Mekeo prophetess Filo (1940–1, Papuan hinterland), for instance, with her claims to have been healed from a snakebite through bottles of 'Jesus water' in the Inawai'a village church and to have seen apparitions of 'Mary heavenly Chief', of Jesus and then of a gun on the church altar, villagers were incited to

---

[6] On how Indigenous fertility cults, sometimes emerging close to contact, could turn into cargo cults, see Trompf 2008a: 174–83.

turn against the Catholic Mission. As Filo was carried around the village in state, her embodiment of spirit-power (*isapu*) made her ripe to be manipulated by Mekeo sorcerers, whose operations were the most threatened by Christian influences. Traditional insignia of A'aisa, the old high deity, 'magic bullets' (*gilis*, very hard bullet-like clay balls traded from the Papuan highland Fuyughe) were displayed, and intensifying dancing and hubbub were manipulated to terrify mission personnel, including nuns. Help was sent for and came in the form of the district resident magistrate, in a truck that many, allegedly, thought bore the anticipated Cargo; but not before a French priest had been gashed, narrowly escaping death from an attacker's conch shell (Fergie 1986: 93–100; Bergendorff 1998: 117–19).

This last incident is emblematic of 1,001 cases in which the socio-religious pasts and future tussled into a climax, unpredictable in terms of any violent outcome. In most cases the majority did not want to be caught up in any fracas. Most Mekeo villages were not involved in the Filo outburst, for a start, and when elsewhere there was talk of rifles arriving from the ancestors, and Cargo to remove dependence on the whites, as prophesied by Sanop of Buka in 1935 (north of Bougainville), only some were persuaded to drill with 'dummy wooden rifles'; although 'the police were to be shot' for interfering, only select leaders had real guns, and in any case most locals preferred waiting for the promises of Sanop's more inspiring predecessor, the pacifist prophet Pako, to be fulfilled; he had thought everyone should just wait to see what the arriving spirits would do (*NGAR* 1935–6: 21–2; Worsley 1970: 126).[7] Still, powerful cultists have certainly been known to bully. During wartime, isolated high-country propagators of the so-called Naked Cult on Espiritu Santo, for example, temporarily 'intimidated' lower-land chiefs into getting their tribes to stop the new practice of wearing clothes (1944–5), at the same time pushing them to destroy all animals and wait for 'America' to bring 'everything good', even an end to death (Miller 1948: 331–2). So-called Batari followers on New Britain, during the Japanese occupation (1942–4), drilled with staves as

[7] On the first case of a prophet captured for 'disturbing the peace', during 1852 in Netherlands New Guinea, see Overweel 1994: 26; and for degrees of turbulence in cargo-type movements there, Kamma 1977: vol. 2, 121–31.

imagined rifles and wore the red circle of Japan's flag on their white armbands. Because the Japanese soldiers said they were 'mixed' people, able to reincarnate, they could always rise up out of the ground to overcome the Australians. Beating unconvinced villagers into submission was known, and they also claimed 'a soldier's right' to violate women (Steinbauer 1971: 140–3; Lattas 1998: 32–43). On tiny Unea (Bali-Vitu Group) in the middle of the Bismarck Sea, the brave young catechist Andrew Devoku had to face a small but terrifying Batari contingent arriving by boat, its officious leader Rave Bakanapuro bent on taking over the island for the Japanese army (whom he proclaimed to be returned ancestors). With the German missionary already imprisoned, Andrew persuaded his flock to keep taking a stand, and when, in early 1944, the Bataris threatened to cut Andrew's legs off – at a time when the Allies were in the process of taking back New Guinea – word got to the police on West New Britain and 120 Batari members were surrounded and arrested. A local pro-Catholic big man was allowed the pleasure of beating Rave from neck to feet into unconsciousness as he lay tied face-down over a box (Oral testimony = OT: Andrew Devoku, 1986).

Only at one point during World War II, however, did anything like a large armed cargo-cult force appear. This was the ABM ('New America' Army) in the Biak-Numfor area (north-coast and island West Irian), formed by followers of Anggganita Menufeur, popular healer-prophetess of Insumbabi Island and acclaimed *konoor* (harbinger and revealer of new riches). At first detained by the Japanese in 1941 for urging local autonomy and framing a new set of laws (prohibiting bloodshed, sea-bathing and eating pork), she returned home in an atmosphere of triumph. Hailed as Mary, and with the regional culture-hero Manggundi (or Manarmakeri) identified with the archangel Gabriel, Anggganita became the centre of new inter-village bonds and high hopes of a miraculous transformation. When she was arrested and not released (May 1942), a huge 'black army' was organized, primarily to get her back from the Japanese but also to destroy anyone hostile to the ABM's cause – including all foreigners, government officials and native Christian preachers. Without effective weaponry, though, the movement's strategist Stephen Simopyaref inspired the ABM soldiers to rely on traditional clubs and magically protective oil, and they died like flies under Japanese firepower and bayonets, with between 600 and 2,000 lives lost. Perhaps this was a case of intended and totally unfulfilled violence, yet as we shall see, such commitment and collective martyrdom became exemplary for later struggles against outside domination (Marjen 1967: 62–5; Kamma 1972: 161–204; Trompf 2008a: 199).

In the postwar period and into that of independence, larger movements formed and had growing reasons to earn respectability, whether they presented as independent churches or as organized affairs powerful enough to float successful electoral candidates (Trompf 1983–4: 51–72, 122–32; 1984: 29–51). In their earlier formations they were noticeably coercive. Famous Madang leader Yali of Sor widened his zone of authority by allowing his 'law-bosses' to do what they wanted by force, through 'rape, intimidation and beating up', and also 'imprisonments', justifying this on the basis of the practices of the colonial officialdom he was replacing (Lawrence 1967: 213–15, 218–20). Similarly, some smaller groups threatened that those who did not join would be 'knifed', even if most took a leaf out of the missionaries' book and urged that good order be maintained (Yagas 1985: 19–21).[8] One movement, Nagriamel (the 'Cycas Palm') in the northern New Hebrides/Vanuatu, later came close to triggering international conflict, although this was not quite what its leader, as a new 'Moses', intended. At the critical juncture when France and Britain were jointly negotiating for Vanuatu's independence in June 1980, Jimmy Stevens, already previously implicated in violent activity on Santo, called for an open all-Islander (*kanak*) uprising – to fulfil his object of setting up a cargo-dreamers' tax haven (with the help of the rightist US Phoenix Foundation) called the Republic of Vemerana. So as to avoid any potential involvement and clashing of French and British troops, the independent Papua New Guinea Defence Force was engaged in its first international engagement to crush what was little more than a voluble independent Church leadership that was blockading unwanted outside interference, in the so-called

---

[8] Yagas shows Kaum, leading the Begesin (or Bagasin) movement, did not follow Yali's views but those of one Tagarab, who sharpened the apocalyptic notions of the Kukuaik as the Japanese appeared (see above, this section); Lawrence 1967: 99–102, 110–16.

'Coconut War' (Hours 1974: 227–42; Shears 1980; Trompf 1980: 29, 33; cf. Abong 2018).

As we can now see, the implications of cargo-cult protestations and spiritual separatisms for large-scale rebellion can hardly be underestimated, but we should draw this section to a close by reckoning with small-scale incidences of violence in Melanesian adjustments and 'new religious' activities that do not make for an easy narrative. Back in the 1880s, for instance, one coastal Mandak clan (New Ireland) chose to sacrifice 'a succession of young children' to obtain European Cargo (perhaps on the principle known in the Lelet Plateau area that one could sacrifice a widow or child to acquire non-ancestral land; Derlon 2008: 106–9, 113). Actualizations or prospects of 'cult killings' for group benefit in cargoist and other new religious movements in Melanesia have occurred from time to time (e.g., Burton-Bradley 1977; cf. 1972; Yagas 1985: 21–2). We find examples of such homicides taking place as part of cargo-cult punitive activity within the Hahalis Welfare society (founded on Buka by John Teosin in 1960). Faceless nocturnal 'hit-men', special killers from among the society's range of 'police, guards, spies and office-bearers', disposed of undesirables and vocal opponents by brutal murder (even of the society's original secretary); the victims were mostly beheaded from behind while bound to coconut stumps cut to shoulder height, in a 'public space' (Trompf 2008a: 234).

The most notorious cult violence in recent times surrounded Manus-born ex-Lutheran seminarian Steven Tari, who gained up to 6,000 followers in Madang highland jungle villages as the white-robed 'Black Jesus' (and often as 'King Yali'), promising riches and well-being to his worshippers (from 2003). Backed by up to 1,000 traditionally armed guards, who burnt and looted opposing Lutheran villages and defended his territory, Tari was also served by accessible pre-pubescent 'flower girls' (a licence Yali had earlier allowed himself with young women). At his trial in 2006 it became clear that Tari had raped various of these girls and used them as so-named 'gates to heaven', but it was harder to prove he killed any of them sacrificially (allegedly by sharing the victims' blood and strips of their flesh with his closest aides, in one case with an assenting mother, in return for the promise of *Kago*). In any case, a violent death awaited him; after escaping from a maximum-security prison, he was castrated and hacked at forty times by angry disaffected villagers on trying to return to his isolated home base. The spiritual independence of these movements had an attraction, but for a more widely reading and normatively Christian PNG public, the distortion of Christian values was both lamentable and deserved severe punishment (OTs: David Maleh et al. in Rello 2019; with Shears 2007).

2.3 Rebellions

Mobilizations of rebellious action can include such religious movements as those we have just considered, yet those termed as a rebellion, revolt, uprising, insurrection, military insurgence, armed independence (or separatist) movement, revolution, or other common epithets (like protest movement or street action, agitation, riot, open tax evasion, strike, civil resistance, group looting and arson, 'luddism' and so on), will usually be read as 'secular-political', and in colonial contexts as pre-political or proto- and micro-nationalist, often without enough attention being paid to their religious content (see esp. Guiart 1951: 81–90; Worsley 1970: 262–4; May 1982; Mrgudovic 2012). This section will have to account for such interpretative proclivities, especially when considering the largest 'hegenomic' configurations in the Pacific in contemporary times. Rebellions took place overwhelmingly in Melanesia and include the following: the Organisasi Papua Merdeka (the Free Papua Movement), starting from 1965 to counter Indonesian control of greater New Guinea's western half; the Front de libération nationale kanake et socialiste (formed in 1984), which worked for a New Caledonian independence that involved renascent indigenous leadership; the Bougainville Revolutionary Army (1988–97), which sought the independence of Bougainville from Australian mining interests and Papua New Guinea's control; and the Malaitan Eagle Force and Isatabu Freedom Movement, which vied with each other over the issue of large Malaitan settlements in and around Honiara, Guadalcanal, in what became known as the Solomons' civil war (1999–2000).

We will leave aside many short-lived eruptions, such as rebel Emboga's seizure of advantage to resist Australian colonials when the Japanese arrived in northern Papua and made rifles available (Waiko 1976). We also set beyond our purview strikes, would-be political parties (including

'Marching' Rule (Maasina Ruru), from 1943), or pro-independence causes (on Hawai'i, French Polynesia, Tonga, Rapanui, etc.) using 'due political process' for their goals. Even Fiji's three renowned coups (in 1987, 2000, and 2006), as endogenous Fijian reactions to rising expatriate Indian power, are marginal to this study. They entailed comparatively moderate levels of violence (cf. Robertson and Tamanisau 1988; Lal and Pretes 2008), not-withstanding the threats in 1987 'to assassinate' the Governor-General or 'burn Suva', voiced by the Taukei (indigenous Fijian radical-nationalist) movement, some random shootings by under-disciplined Fijian soldiery and the hostage-taking of selected parliamentarians by coup-leader George Speight in 2000, with the menace of his supporters' 'extrapunitive' attacks against Indian farms (Field et al. 2005: 73–191; Thomson 2008: 146–8; Ramesh 2010: 66–126; with OT from Revd R. Udy, 28 May 2021). As Fiji became a Republic and a 'secular state' in 2011 (Fiji Constitution (ch. 1): 1; 4), it may now look as though Fijian indigenous/Indian relations are essentially political and ethnic issues. Admittedly, Taukei stalwarts strenu-ously uphold the three time-honoured 'pillars of Fijian Society'. In their terms, these are: the native Islanders (*I taukei*), descendants from lost Israelite tribes and take precedence over latecomers (a rejection of multi-culturalism); the Great Council of Chiefs (suspended 2007); Christianity (checking other religions' (especially Hinduism's) pretensions) essentially as mediated by the Methodist Church (although this was temporarily side-lined by Catholic-educated PM Frank Bainimarama's 2006 coup) (Ryle 2005; yet cf. Niukula 1992; Newland 2015). Thus, future serious unrest and outbursts of violence connected to religion can hardly be ruled out, but there are currently more avenues in Fiji by which religion can be deployed as a social constrainer rather than as a reason to fight (cf. Fraenkel and Firth 2007).

However, let us go back to do some historical homework. When Peter Hempenstall penned his important *Pacific Islanders under German Rule: A Study in the Meaning of Colonial Resistance*, he focused on three aspects: Polynesia's Samoan chiefs threatening to reclaim political and economic control (in 1893 and especially 1908–9); the 'frenzied' reaction on Micronesia's Pohnpei (1901), using bodily protective 'magic oil', against the imposition of a plantation economy; and on Melanesians' reactions to the alienation of their land for the purposes of settling and planting along the coasts of northern New Britain and Madang (esp. 1893, 1900, 1902 and 1904) (Hempenstall 1978: 55–65, 95–105 (with quotation), 129, 131, 145–51, 179–94; cf. Hempenstall and Rutherford 1984: esp. 18–43, 119–46. But of course, religious factors always lurked. Samoan chieftainship was 'hedged about with divinity' (*mana*) (Stuebel 1895: 778–80), and land is enshrouded with sacrality in the Pacific. Pohnpe's most sacred site, the mysterious stone city Nan Madol, was dedicated in legend 'to the Honoured Spirit of the Land' (Nahnisohnsapw), embodied in the great Seawater Eel; the island's name (*Pohn-pei*) already referred to offerings being made to him 'upon a Stone Altar'. For Ponapeans, matters were complicated by German efforts in the 1900s to encourage Protestantism where Catholics had been long established on the island, the latters' faith having been introduced by the Spanish (Petersen 1993; Athens 2009; Hanlon 2019: 3–25), with the prior settling of American Protestants (from the 1850s) having already been used as an excuse for armed resistance to Spanish rule in 1890 (using sorcery-based 'supernatural assistance') (Hanlon 1990: 113–14). As for Melanesia, throughout the region, land inheritance normally derived from the communality shared between ancestors and the living, with the introduced general concept of 'God' synthesizing their cosmic sense of their 'right to their islands' (e.g., Narokobi 1988: esp. 8; Sharp 1993: Scott 2007: esp. 15; Longgar 2008, with Sharp 1993: 121).

When we come to look at significant expressions of violent resistance in the Pacific, then, despite the tendency of political analysts and news commentators to over-politicize matters, we should also take account of Pacific Islander spiritual assumptions. Setting aside minor affairs in earlier colonial contexts,[9] let the 1878–9 New Caledonian insurrection set the tone. With Grande Terre on the way to becoming 'France's Australia', this revolt was all about the loss of the indigenous peoples' land, resources, health and

---

[9] Thinking here, for example, of the continuation of the Māori land wars in the Parihaka protests (1870s–1880s); the 1889 Hawaiian rebellion (led by Col. Robert Wilcox and Robert Boyd) to protect Islander interests under British rule; and the 1914 repossessions and cult-rebellion of the 'prophetess' Angata on Rapanui against Scottish settler domination.

freedom: the French military *gouverneurs* had made lands available to settlers (*colons*) – French, Anglophone, other South Sea Islander and emancipating convicts – by creating and further delimiting native land reserves, and facilitating white settlement even to the point of shipping in prefabricated houses. The *gouverneurs* took little action against the destruction of indigenous agricultural land by introduced ranch cattle, and they imposed hated *corvée*-labour on able-bodied villagers (for road-building, etc.) (Godard et al. 1978: 342–54, 435; Kemelfield 1976; Dousset-Leenhardt 1978). The area where most of the insurrectionary action took place lay along the south-west coast and hinterland, and along the La Foa River valley the rebels had the benefit of the leadership of the high Chief Atea. Atea was a cunning strategist, who co-ordinated a sufficient number of allied and previously enemy tribes, bolstered by his fearful son, an impish four-foot-high sorcerer 'of the most powerful description' and with decisive 'influence over the natives', in a culture widely feared for its *sorcellerie* (*SMH* 10 Oct. 1878: 8; 18 Jul. 1878: 7; 7 Nov. 1878: 7; *Maryborough Chronicle*, 20 Jul. 1878: 5). Unlike today, in this context the main role of the sorcerer, as 'soul killer', was to direct spiritual power against external foes, in this case foreigners and their abettors (Métais 1967: esp. 137–40). For tribes supporting him, Atea projected the enemy as unworthily 'materialistic and profane' for spurning dialogue, reciprocity and 'the highest values' traditionally upheld by his island's peoples (Dousset-Leenhardt 1978: 112; Métais 1988; Connell 1987: 66–7). The fierce massacres that occurred, wild-cattle-killing, torching of sugar mills and white properties and the mounting of a cross-tribal *canaque* force ready to threaten the new capital of Nouméa, did not issue, however, from 'nascent nationalist sentiments' but from collective despair over injustice (thus Connell 1987: 69, as against Guiart 1968: 109–10).

When this insurrection was put down, with over 1,200 dead (most of these casualties not immediately involved in the conflict) (Saussol 1979: 242), all preceding outbursts of anti-colonial resistance paled into insignificance beside it, and in the long run it was recognized for New Caledonian human relations that 'more lives had been lost' in the violence of 1878 'than would ever be lost again in subsequent struggles' (Connell 1987: 70–83). What allowed the French their victory, though, was their better armed force with its troops and police, the release of imprisoned Algerian rebels only too willing to take on *les sauvages* and the assistance of certain *canaque* groups that were advantaged or treated more respectfully under the regime than were other groups (Godard et al. 1978: vol. 1: 407–32). After punishments by displacement of rebel tribes, subsequent efforts at resistance, particularly in the north during 1917, were quickly arrested, with the reprisals' 'long duration and the larger scale of mortalities' inflicted on indigenes, and the withdrawal of privileges associated with those reprisals, being more severe than the effects of comparable punishment measures anywhere else in Melanesia (Connell 1993: 228).

Demoralization and a kind of 'Christian village' domestication have long prevailed on New Caledonia's main island since these disturbances) (Wete 1991). The combined injection of liberation theology and socialist politics affecting the formation of the pan-*canaque* Front de liberation nationale kanake et socialiste (FLNKS) in 1984 is indicative of a relative avoidance of unfruitful violence, in favour of propaganda for independence. The Front achieved momentum from the 1970s to regain traditional lands by demonstrations, boycotts and planned incidents of non-cooperation, stirred by ex-priest Jean-Marie Tjibaou, son of a Hienghène chief in the north-east (Anova-Ataba 1985; Connell 1993: 228–40). Along the way, though, matters spilled over into physical assaults, most notoriously in the 1988 rebel seizure of gendarmes as hostages (on Ouvea, Loyalties) and the assassination of Tjibaou himself (and his deputy Yeiwene), both masterminded by radical separatist Djubelly Wea, who wanted no peace talks with France. The FLNKS, itself faction-ridden as a result of trying to represent twenty-eight highly colonized cultures, sat between a more conciliatory Union Calédonienne and the secular leftist Front de Libération (*New York Times*, 25 May 1989: A5; Robie 1989: 270; Trompf 2008a: 352; cf. Naepels 2017: 235–80). To date, left-leaning hopes for independence have been twice dashed in plebiscites, and serious rebel actions have stalled by paradoxes of democracy.

By contrast, the operations of West Papua's Organisasi Papua Merdeka (OPM) and those organs of rebellion in the Solomons region (soon to be assessed) have engaged in armed military force, though it will naturally be our point for these cases that fighting for their respective causes did not exclude religious elements. In all of them we find a sacralizing of land or people and the justifying of violent action as an essential recourse for justice. If in New Caledonia independence strugglers had no real 'legacy of martyrdom', West Papuans upholding the OPM could find it in the tragic attempts of the ABM to overcome the Japanese soldiery (1942) (Ondawame 2006, and above Section 2.2), inspiring them in their part-militarily organized – if utterly one-sided – struggle against yet another Asian power (the Indonesians having patently rigged the 1969 UN Act of Free Choice by paying off chiefs to accept their takeover) (Utrecht 1978). The flag of the Land of the Morning Star, accepted by the Dutch as a territorial symbol, had in a 1971 Proclamation become the emblem of would-be *national* unity 'with the help and blessing of God Almighty', along with the national anthem (finishing with the words: 'Thank you, Lord on High, this land is mine'), composed by the Dutch missionary Izaak Kijne (Tanggahma 2012; Kijne 1993–4; with Neilson 2021: 392). The potential nation was assumed to be a Christian one, not part of the world's most populous Muslim country next door. As a wider political movement, the OPM's actions are marked by provocatively public flag-waving and anthem-singing (prohibited by Indonesia), but its guerrilla wing(s) could hardly be disavowed (its flags often carried the insignia of a bird of paradise on crossed bayoneted rifles and cutlasses). Jacob Prai, the region's most prominent military strategist (now exiled to Sweden) and a Christian socialist, insisted that West Papuan churches should play an integral part on the freedom cause (even though their ministers increasingly serve mixed-ethnic congregations and receive directives to uphold the law of the land (cf. Rom. 13:1–7) (Campbell 2016). The OPM's fighters are scattered and poorly armed, and as with New Caledonia's FLNKS, they have often split into factions (Blaskett 1993: Braithwaite 2010). Various units have favoured less brutal methods that appear to keep to the majority's Christian code: to avoid as much bloodshed as possible; to damage the opposition's equipment over carrying out military assault, where possible; to care well for captives; and to refrain from rape and looting. Otherwise, its fighters are warned that an Indonesian bullet will 'justly find' them (Fairio 1985: 4–6, with OT: Jul. 1985). In the important 1985 (Port) Vila Declaration (actually facilitated by telephone calls in the author's own home), relative unity in terms of the OPM's objectives was secured, as well as an operating base in Vanuatu. By 2003, having achieved little success in the field and after bad reactions by villagers to guerrilla filching of their resources, the movement chose pacifist political tactics, and its flag-raisings sometimes included that of modern Israel, to identify with the Jews' ancient struggles in the Holy Land (Ondawame 2003: 107; H. Myrttinen 2015). Human rights violations by Indonesian forces, however – indeed at times genocidal-looking oppression (Wing and King 2005), including in and around the world's largest gold and silver mine at Freeport in the south-west – brought about a resuscitation of military action. Of note have been the agitant Terianus Santo, who formed a better-organized Liberation Army (the TPNPB, in 2012), and Victor Yeimo, spokesman of the West Papua National Committee, who was arrested as a suspected 'terrorist' in 2021, while wearing a T-shirt with the motto 'Trust in the Lord with All Your Heart'. A month earlier, separatist guerrillas had shot dead Indonesia's top intelligence officer (Brig. Gen. Karya Nugraha), and in reaction hundreds of troops poured into West Papua, historically a sign that human rights would be violated.[10]

On the far-eastern edges of PNG, the Bougainville crisis was sparked by 'Luddite' action against Rio Tinto's copper mine (BCL, or Bougainville Copper Limited) at Panguna on Nasioi land, the Nasioi being 'the world's first indigenous people . . . to shut down a multinational mining venture', after extraction tailings had polluted the Jaba river and its adjacent lands (Wilson 2018: 2). The assault on electricity-bearing pylons and machinery resulted in police action, but tit-for-tat engagements between saboteurs and authorities soon escalated into 'Melanesia's first [large-scale] "payback war"' (Trompf 2008a: 353). In attempts to place the role of religion in this conflict, the initiator of the anti-BCL outbreak, Francis Ona, has been contrastingly represented on the one hand as a devout Marianist (in heavily Marist Catholic Mission country), by Anna-Karina Hermkens (2013), and on the other as more 'cargoist', a view that takes into account the influence on

---

[10] On Yeimo, using online: https://asiapacificreport.nz/2021/05/11; on Nugrah's killing, and so on, N. L. C.Yewen, 'Indonesia's Restive Papua Region, etc.', online: www.scmp.com/week-asia/politics/article3139577.

him of the shadowy Demien Damen (and one that I myself argue for). Damen had developed a cargo cult in 1962 among the Nasioi (who had a long history of such activity), and advocated keeping up a Catholic front while covertly working for 'the empowerment of the ancestors' to secure freedom for *Me'ekamui* 'the sacred [is]land' (of Bougainville) and redress the inequalities that had increased exponentially since the mine opened in 1972 (Trompf 2004: 233; and for background Ogan 1974: 117–21; Sipari 1985).

In this author's own left-field move to avert Australia away from engaging in war on behalf of its multinational company in 1988, I admittedly overdid Ona's psychological instability (and wrongly accused him of having had a violent past) (Trompf n.d.), but in any case the formation of the Bougainville Revolutionary Army (BRA) under Joseph Kabui was not long in coming, along with its attacks on plantations and government stations as foreign threats. The PNG Defence Force, or PNGDF, was thereafter deployed for its second outstanding operation; this time in a veritable 'borderland war' (with hawkish leadership in the PNGDF wanting to place 'a large bounty on Ona's head') (Braithwaite et al. 2010a: 24). The leech-ridden slipperiness of the terrain made conventional army operations impossible. Helicopters granted by Australia strictly for transport purposes, and with New Zealand pilots, came to be used for airborne attacks (including the desperate dropping of sorcery bundles by Tolai defence personnel!). The intensifying struggle became lethal, with around 1500 combatants killed and some 17–20,000 extra casualties (May and Spriggs 1992: 173–180). The earlier Bougainvillean complaints that BCL profits were being syphoned off inequitably to the rest of PNG escalated into a fight for survival, while the old mainland-PNGers' lurking disdain towards the decidedly black-skinned inhabitants of the North Solomons Province turned into bitter racism (Mamak et al. 1979: 69–75). Enmity metamorphosed from the tribal to the regional level, and so for that reason the outsider PNGDF assailants were set a professional and somewhat religionless task. By contrast, saving *Me'ekamui* was the sustaining ideology of the insider freedom fighters, and it is clear Ona and the BRA leadership appropriated the Legion of Mary and the Our Lady of Mercy movement (the former having been banned in Bougainville for becoming too cargo-cultish) to proselytize for allegiance to the BRA (Hermkens

2015). The most powerful religious narratives in the whole history of the Melanesian wars, though, are surely those of the Christian families and village groups caught in the cross-fire, who somehow survived, or gave their lives to save others (Trompf n.d.).[11] Those Buka and Bougainville islanders who wanted special autonomy, but without war, were particularly vulnerable, and would in the end be crucial to the notably Church-influenced reconciliation that took place (2001) (Howley 2002). Not long before the time of writing, and despite dissident threats of derailment (*Post-Courier*, 16 Jul. 2019), 97 per cent of North Solomonese chose independence in a referendum, a freedom yet to be realized (it was put off until 2027).

As for the Central Solomons civil war, it erupted because of interregional (or inter-island) violence when collaborating villagers on Guadalcanal (where the capital Honiari is located) turned on the immigrant and squatter settlements of the Malaitans, who seemed to be visibly rising in numbers, were hungry for land near the city, and were perceived as aggressive when visible as street gangs or drifters (both groups nicknamed 'Masta Liu') (Bennett 2002). Key local masterminds of reaction were Harold Keke, a daily-praying, self-declared prophet calling his people to 'the promised land', in a strange liaison with the formidable Stanley Koani (aka 'Satan') (Bohane 2013). The Guadalcanal Liberation Front (GLF) they both helped organize targeted Malaitan civilians (over 150 being killed, mainly women, with rape and sexual crimes involved) and extorted unlawful rent payments on pain of death. At a later point Keke eventually had a Catholic priest (who was also an MP) executed as a spy, as well as seven indigenous Anglican Melanesian Brothers who had tried to mediate for peace (Carter 2006). By early 1999, two emergent forces were locking horns in and around Honiara: the Isatabu Freedom Movement (IFM, incorporating the GLF – now redesignated as the Guadalcanal Revolutionary Army and bent on saving Guadalcanal) versus the Malaitan Eagles Force (MEF), defending their fellow Malaitan settlers (20,000 of whom, mainly second-generation dwellers in Honiara, fled back to Malaita from the scene of the conflict). The

---

[11] Trompf n.d. (three archived folders, including 1988 articles in *The Australian*; 'Open Letter to Francis Ona', in Tok Pisin, for *Arawa Bulletin* 1988; and interview notes of survivors' stories).

national government was caught by surprise and ill-equipped to handle the situation; and in 2000, after failing to secure international assistance and control the 'ethnic tensions', the frustrated MEF and the (Malaitan-dominated) police force took Prime Minister Bart Ulufa'alu hostage (while he was Malaitan himself, he belonged to the Catholic minority there; Kenilorea 2008: 343–5). This coup-like action brought on rioting (and the burning of Honiara's Chinatown), along with a confusing tussle to fill the vacant top office. The two contenders were both Choiseul Islanders (from the west of the country); the SDA son of a missionary to PNG – who won – and the founding Moderator of the United Church! Surprisingly, when the Commonwealth (mostly Australian) police of the Regional Assistance Mission to Solomon Islands (RAMSI) intervened, the conflict subsided. But reconciliation was clinched only after the utterly recalcitrant Keke had been arrested in his cultish hideout in Guadalcanal's deeply forested Weathercoast, and despite the indigenous police–MEF alliance to control the country's most effective armoury (Fraenkel 2004: 53–94, 139–87; Moore 2004; Dinnen 2009; Droogan and Waldek 2015: esp. 294; cf. *The Australian*, 17–18 Mar. 2001: 11).

In our attempts to understand this violence, which would leave 200 dead and 11,000 displaced and included 5,700 human rights violations, 1,413 torture cases and more than 60 rapes, we should reckon with the conditioning effects of religious factors in strengthening island identities. The IFM cause was based more plainly on the defence of ancestrally held territory; the Malaitans had a heritage of sacred land, were proud of their resistance to blackbirding and British colonialism (with the alternative government of 'Marching Rule'), and have widely held that they had brought the Solomons a special connection to ancient Israel and were perhaps even descended from the Israelites, their ancestors having voyaged to the islands from the Holy Land (Moore 2017; Akin 2013; with Keesing 1982: 49–50; Timmer 2012). Acting on resentments of a regional, not tribal, character gave momentum to cycles of revenge that threatened nationhood. Socio-mental devices to satisfy grievances inherited from the pluri-cultural past (traditional payback principles, stories of righteous Old Testament victories, the possibility of access to powerful weapons that local people had been debarred from using since colonial times) trampled over the Peace of Christ and national law and order, producing the first civil war of the Pacific. The churches, despite their denominational differences, had to play a crucial role in reasserting the higher spiritual unity of the one faith and the mystery of forgiveness in a sacred *communio*, necessary for underpinning the Solomons as a nation among many nations (cf. Braithwaite et al. 2010b: 81–94; Jeffrey 2017: esp. 113–39), while grievances hung on, with bursts of rioting in Honiara (in 2006, 2014, and 2019).

Generally, as we can see, Pacific Islander religious movements and rebellions have taken the old defence of confined sacred tribal land to wider and wider territories of concern, with spreading alliances to bond against a common threat and adopting causes with regional, separatist, even nationalist foci that can be hallowed in distinct ways, appropriating Christian and Western national talk of justice and goodness. To illustrate further, just before PNG independence, Orokaivan campaigners in northern Papua stressed the need for a new 'togetherness' and 'close communal' life, building new villages with streets named after tribes, cultural heroes, and great ancestors, before starting to create their own great cooperative. Then came their February 1975 march on Port Moresby as the Papuan Fighters Republican Army, along the renowned Kokoda Trail, to express their frustration and join others who wanted a free Papua (then still hoping to remain separate from New Guinea and its turbulent central highlanders; Jojoga Opeba 1993: 267–72, 276–84). Not surprisingly, in the Catholic ambience of central Bougainville, supporters of Francis Ona stewed over Christian notions of a 'just war', and when autonomy was at last in sight, Francis himself tried clinching his superiority (in 2004) by peremptorily crowning himself 'king of Me'ekamui', shortly before he died in 2005 (Hermkens 2015: 45–7).[12]

2.4 Developments from Traditional Modes of Violence

We are now left to ponder the large mass of unmanageable materials that illustrate the persistence and modification of traditional patterns of violence into current times. Here we discuss as key topics in their turn: the

---

[12] More strictly political movements bringing tensions include the Mataungan League (New Britain), the Kabisawali People's Government (Trobriands), the Highlands Liberation Front (Melanesia), the Samoan Mau movement (1926–38), and actions towards integrating the two Samoas (wider Pacific).

continuance of group fighting under new guises; gangs; modern guns in conflicts; sorcery and witchcraft after contact; and custodial punitions.

2.4.1 Neo-traditional Fighting

Starting with the *persistence and modifications of tribal warfare*, we find that, quite expectedly, Melanesia will receive the most focus in this section. This is because the dampening of old patterns of violence has taken longer and occurred unevenly due to the fact that various 'first-contact' situations took place only after World War II, which in itself was a huge disruption that caused reversion to incidents of headhunting (Kroef 1959: 152–4) on some Jahray people (south-west Papua). Thus in some pockets of dense jungle terrain and highly populous highland valleys in Melanesia, entrenched local enmities have tended to flare up if some damaging incident 'scratches the wounds', and police are called in (Fig. 4.) As we began tracing diachronically in our previous Element (Trompf 2021a: 55–9), armed violence has been affected by socio-religious change. Even acceptance of a mission could

Figure 4 Dutch colonial official and assistant forestall intra-tribal conflict over a bigman's second wife, fringe Dani, West Papua, 1961
Source: Illustrated London News *13 Jan. 1962.*

be used as cover for slaughter, as when in 1954 some revenge-hungry Jipair Asmat from within Catholic villages (densely tropical southwest West Papua) invited new converts over from a recently established post at Ayam and suddenly let fly, killing thirty-one of them and traumatizing the missionary into leaving forever (Boelaars and Vriens 1986: vol. 2, II.11– 15, 20–1). This is an example of how ongoing conflict incurs collateral casualties, destabilizing fragile religious efforts at 'integral development' and making nation-building arduous. Elsewhere in Melanesia the persistence of conflict has its own attractions and conveniences for solidary interests. In the only area where the author has himself documented field fighting, on the Wahgi/Chimbu central highland borderland in 1980, with the Kumai and Endugla tribes facing off, it soon became plain that clashes were reserved for the Christmas holiday period, when able-bodied young men were to hand, with one of my chief informants explaining that he had returned from his seminary schooling in coastal Madang 'to fight for his country' (which meant both his own tribe and all the Wahgi on their territorial edge). I found the local Catholic priest fuming over why his parish had to display this kind of unrelenting behaviour (Trompf 2008a: 325–7). Under such circumstances, with easier relationships between tribes now making it more possible that you might face an in-law on the field, it may be preferable to give one's shield some individualized marking not used traditionally!

Of course, it has been up to missionaries and administrators to utilize negotiating skills and come up with imaginative devices to secure good order. Among the Chimbu in the 1980s, for instance, the African American bishop Caesar imposed an interdict (or prohibition from partaking of the Holy Sacrament) on any Catholic lineage or clan that initiated or abetted a tribal fight (cf. Young 1986). Among the Sawi (neighbouring the Asmat to the north), who treacherously enticed in neighbouring guests and feted and then killed them (even reworking 'church talk' to make Judas their hero), Canadian Protestant missionaries Don and Carol Richardson unwittingly brought about a shift in relations. By holding up their own infant son on first engaging with the Sawi they made an indelible token of peace, and developed an effective missiology of Christ as 'Peace Child' thereafter (Richardson 1976). But, of course, both intent and space prevent this book from covering the history and theory of peacemaking and process in Oceania (Trompf 2008a: esp. 97–107; Strathern and Stewart 2011; Wiessner and Pupu 2012: 1651–4; Lohmann 2014), and here we shall consider such matters only insofar as they throw light on phenomena of violence.

As a result of pressures of social change, traditional revenge syndromes can bend into shapes that would have occurred only exceptionally in the 'times before'. Thus in New Guinea highland areas, the increase in population (due to disease containment) put pressure on land, and *land disputes* became a crucial basis for tribal wars (especially among the Mae Enga and Chimbu) in ways not known before; and while introduced plantations in the highlands (coffee, tea, pyrethrum, etc.) allowed these areas entrance into the cash economy, they also took away arable terrain (Meggitt 1977: 16–21; Trompf 2008a: 28, 329–30). As a result of all this, the unspeakable happened: *intra*-tribal war. Clans that had formerly kept a united tribal front, not lifting lethal weapons but only blunt instruments in internal group quarrels, began turning on each other more ruthlessly (in the highlands this starting among the Gumini, a Chimbu grouping). Under the colonial conditions that had been imposed, moreover, while tribal war had been effectively prohibited, undercover one-to-one homicides between groups kept up old sores, and increasingly an aggrieved party would bide their time before taking one or two lives. Whether perpetrated by one or many, under state rules such killings were punishable as murder.[13]

With the advent of various non-traditional fixtures – new regional or district or provincial boundaries, political parties and their vying candidates, and special points of rivalry (in sports, regional shows, etc.), came unprecedented occasions for violence and individual killings, particularly in the PNG highlands. Two new fragile highland provinces were created in grassroots reactions to the effect of tribal violence on development. First, Hela Province split off from the Southern Highlands in 2012 under the name

---

[13] To trace resurgent highland tribal warfare from 1974 (on a relative lull) use the indices in IASER 1978–9: for 1972, (pp.) 129–31; for 1973, 135–130; 1974, 134–6; 1976, 118–19; 1977, 158–64; 1978, 186–8. For the Eastern Highlands, Schwoerer (2017: 317–36) puts the resurgence mainly down to sorcery accusations; of relevance is Trompf 2008a: 434, on burials too near to watercourses.

of their shared great Ancestor and with common fertility rituals, to avoid involvement in hotspots continuing around Mendi since the 1990s and looming in the remote Sugu Valley (which became serious after 2013). And, second, Jiwaka Province broke off in the same year, with the 'more settled' Wahgi separating from the turbulent Melpa tribes and the 'Wild West' conditions of Mount Hagen township (capital of the Western Highlands Province).[14] Since districts and provinces have become increasingly connected by public transport in PNG, individual killngs can either reflect ancient enmities (scores being settled between tribes by despatching vulnerable individuals in urban settings, plantations, or mines) or those between larger regional groupings. If a Sepik driver from a particular culture kills someone on the Highlands Highway, for example, and this death has not been avenged on the perpetrator, any Sepik at all wherever they are will be warned to be on high alert until a 'reply death' occurs. In this context, all Sepik River people act as *wantoks* (Tok Pisin: they 'talk the same language [contextually]'), even if they have their own intra-regional conflict issues, while the highland lineage or clan 'owning the quarrel' remain *wanpis* ('not having or necessarily expecting support'); but if word has it that certain aggrieved Sepiks themselves seek revenge, paradoxically, as many highlanders as learn of the conflict will paradoxically share their common bond through gossip (and in fear of coastal *sanguma* sorcery) until the trouble hopefully blows over (*i go pas*) for any given town or district. The sense of sacred obligation to sustain one's security circle (following Trompf 2021a) has been extended, though with lessened pressure the further the reach. In an urban context, blood feuding has emerged between geographically quite separate migrant groups competing for the same opportunities (as with the Papuan highland Tauade and central highland

---

[14] For Hela: 'Hela Province', *Wikipedia*, https://en.wikipedia.org/wiki/Hela_Province, cf. Matthew 1996; with ABC News, 'Tribal Fighting in PNG Highlands Was "Unspeakable Violence"', *ABC News* (13 Nov. 2013) (Sugu Valley), www.abc.net.au/news/2013-11-13/an-png-leader-says-tribal-killings-27unspeakable-violence27/5089786. For Jiwaka: 'Jiwaka Province', *Wikipedia*, https://en.wikipedia.org/wiki/Jiwaka_Province; and see OT: Michael Wandil (2014, as administrator from one western highlands province to another).

Chimbu seeking rubbish-collecting contracts). In the context of large development projects, ferocious conflict can erupt when one clan apparently gains better access to riches than others. The broadest groups involving revenge killings in PNG would be coastals *versus* highlanders (usually in close working proximity, as in a city or suburb) or Papuans *versus* New Guineans. And this pattern translates itself in wider Melanesia (thus Guadalcanals *versus* Malaitans); though in wider Oceania, such rivalries lead to less 'rough justice' and both Church and legal authorities (in some cases eager to preserve the aura of severity around chiefs and their councils), are strong in deterring such escalations (Trompf 2008a: 334–5, 338–51; with Stewart and Strathern 2002b): esp. 1–45, 135–72).

As has partly been intimated, restrained violence is most obviously accepted within agnatic lineages, clans, tribes, totem groups, affinal linkages, and (where applicable) some phratries, which compose an individual's security circle or parts thereof. In general, the Church is presented in the Pacific as a new and ultimate security circle. In denominational spheres of influence, a widening of safe passageways far from traditionally confined locales was provided by Christian hospitality, and reciprocal gift-giving was endowed with different auras of respect; in Protestant countries these were often around indigenous or Islander pastors, who were key in binding peaceful solidarity. But of course there were denominational clashes; before the mid-1950s these occurred not uncommonly between Catholics and Protestants; from the 1920s, between mainline Church members and sectarians (such as SDAs), and from the 1970s, between 'revivalists' (charismatics, Pentecostalists, etc.). With some exceptions, brawls were fought with fists and blunt objects, but property damage could be done.

Looking across the Pacific, in 1898 on Pohnpe's Awak peninsula in Micronesia, for instance, 'several parties joined in an attack ... to drive out all Catholics' (and support the powerful Protestant pastor Henry Nanpei), and wholesale fire damage to Catholic Mission properties could not be forestalled before a Spanish man-of-war arrived (Hezel 1971: 41a). On Tonga's main island of Nuku'alofa, recurrent violence has long surrounded students from the main high schools. With King George Tupou I having inaugurated the independent 'Free Wesleyan' church in 1875, Tupou College (Wesleyan Mission-founded and the oldest secondary school in the Pacific Islands, since back in 1866) has become locked in bitter rivalry with the impressive royally established Tonga High School (begun 1947). Scrapping in the streets and at sporting venues has been recurrent, involving occasional deaths and frequent police action in what has become a 'national crisis' (Lee 2018: 126–8). Significantly, at schools in Melanesia homicidal revenge, say on a bully, has usually seemed out of place, and most interdenominational skirmishes have been played out with fisticuffs (e.g., Saunana 1980: 50), yet sporadically, also with arson. In 2014, however, Lae became a hotspot in which interregional payback killings were carried out in a secular urban school setting (Anon. 2014).[15]

2.4.2 Gangs

Found in cities and towns, and issuing from plantations, is *the problem of gangs*. Inequities under social change, particularly unemployment among youths in urban areas, have produced listless school drop-outs without direction, susceptible to joining small coteries and ready to engage in crimes such as breaking and entering and street-gang skirmishing over 'turf', especially in the sprawling squatter settlements, most noticeably in PNG's Port Moresby and Lae since around 1980. The gang is a special modification of the tribe, because a leader, more experienced and perhaps older, can instruct younger members (generally in their early teens) in group rules, rituals and symbolic markers. Gang markers of neo-tribal identity include tattoos, skin-cutting for blood brotherhood, evocative names ('Japs', 'Mafia', 'Goipex 105', etc.) and violent initiatory acts, such as supervised gang rape, most notoriously in Moresby against white women in 1985 (Trompf 2008a: 331–81; Dinnen 1998). Vicious consequences follow if any relatives of rape victims try to take revenge into their own hands (*The National* (PNG), 27 Dec. 2019). Gang solidarity is inspired by the behaviour of gangsters seen in outdoor public film-shows; the exhilaration of the members' exploits in rival gang 'show-downs' (Fig. 5) or successful 'break-ins'; having access to safe

[15] For a general perspective, Strathern 1993: 190–246; Trompf 2008a: 291–303.

Figure 5 Members of two rival gangs scuffle outside a trade store, Bululo, Morobe Province, PNG
Source: Photograph by the author (1993)

hiding places; and in some cases, by feeling more valued as a result of working to protect the interests of powerful paymasters, politicians not excluded (Trompf 1994: 34, 36–7; Dinnen 2001). In political, not just religious terms, intriguingly, the conversion of leading 'rascals' (*raskol*) from the path of crime has been a striking phenomenon, as a redirecting of tough leadership (Trompf 1996: 220–5). Bill Skate, a reformed gang leader from Moresby's oldest squatter settlement – if he commands his 'members to kill, they kill' – inspirationally rose to the city's governorship and then PNG's prime ministership. His direct style clinched an end to the frustrating Bougainville war, after his predecessor had been exposed for trying to engage Sandline mercenaries and after Moresby had consequently experienced weeks of student protests, rioting, and looting, and had narrowly excaped a military coup (Mar. 1997) (*SMH* 4 Jan. 2005; Aust. Govt. *Hansard* 1 Dec. 1997; O'Callahan 1999).

While youth group violence can be better contained on smaller islands, gangs there can become proudly 'neo-national', as when Micronesian Nauruan thugs (particularly the self-ascribed 'Mongrel Mob') take on foreign asylum seekers who have been let out into the community (*Guardian*, 7 Oct. 2015). Or again, as a result of international migration, the Tongan 'Crisps' and 'Sons of Samoa' (formed in Australia, New Zealand, and the USA) (Lee 2003: 300; James 2002: 144), and Cook Island groups in New Zealand, enjoy notoriety in the press. Polynesian gangs are formed due to lack of employment, attracting 'urban castaways' to a 'brotherhood of Polynesian youth', with intricate tattoo identities, who engage in drug peddling (the latter activity playing out further in street crime and violence, as the drugs are sold to offer para-religious experiences; Loomis 1984: 158–64. See, more generally, Lee 2019).

With our mention of drugs we can hardly bypass the issue of alcohol, a favourite object of gang theft, an inflaming factor in many conflicts, and an all-too-ready subverter of peacemaking. In the rural areas, especially in the PNG highlands, party politics can take on aspects of clashing clan loyalties, as youths are paid to add threatening aspects to campaigning (whether explicit or implicit), and voters are bribed with free alcohol. In Wayne Warry's useful study of Chuave politics in the Chimbu region, we see that continuing tribal conflict (which, to reiterate, we read as part of traditional 'religious life') feeds into rivalry between candidates, who campaign for the interests of their tribes, so that a victory at the polls means the diversion of infrastructural development to those allied to the winners, the losers face potential neglect until the next round of voting, and old wounds are salted. There is not only the danger of conflict erupting at the ballot box or after electoral results have been announced, but of allegations of misconduct, corruption, and electioneering by thuggery and 'threat of the gun', that produce political homicides (Warry 1987: 21–4, 35–6, 50–79, 262–5, 272; cf. Standish 2003 for central Chimbu, where up to 100 highlanders were killed during the 2002 polling campaign).[16]

---

[16] But Warry stresses signs of new political leaders using healthier negotiating skills for campaigning, and he highlights how influential Church women can ease matters (chs. 5–7). Extrajudicial political killings in spite of court acquittals need

2.4.3 New Guns

Continuing tribal and neo-tribal violence has been seriously affected (by national and provincial consensuses 'for the worse' by the *growing availability of technologically sophisticated weaponry*. Apart from places where the odd musket and then shotgun was to hand, long-handled iron axes were the main and formidable addition to arsenals in the ongoing tribal fighting for most of the twentieth century. In Melanesia, where weapons could easily be left behind on a rocky battlefield, the loss of guns could backfire dangerously. As traditional field fighting subsided across the board, machetes and steel knives or axes proved handier, gang youths stole and made use of a variety of handyman's tools, and the modern arsenal of the OPM in West Papua was badly deficient. When the author and his missionary doctoral student raised the alarm (in a 1997 *Current Affairs Bulletin*) about sophisticated long-range rifles being used in the New Guinea highland conflict, fears were awakening that the gun-running which had affected the Bougainville crisis would extend to regions where very old styles of warfare were still continuing (Bieniek and Trompf 1997: 27–8; followed up by Standish 1999–2000: 25; Trompf 2008: 350–1, 354, etc.). Thereafter, in a phenomenon first noticeable in high West Enga country, the owners of a quarrel could pick off an enemy across a whole valley using a telescopically fitted rifle (whether for traditional tribal reasons, or perhaps due to a personal squabble over gold diggings in and around the Porgera mine) (see Fig. 6). Word will get around, of course, as to a suspect gun-possessor, as in West Enga (where, like a Viking, one carries precautionary weapons on the way to church and leaves them outside at the narthex porch). But by the time police arrive at a potential culprit's settlement, the gun will have been passed on into the bush. Sometimes an increase in the number of arms actually makes it easier to locate the sources of the group's firearms.[17] When in 1999 the MEF started uncovering leftover stocks of US weaponry on Malaita from World War II, it was crucial for peacemaking that the caches were publicly located and sacred promises made never to open them again. But overall, the spread and prospective further dissemination of

assessing, noting the 1992 murder of Hela founder-figure Aruru Matiable, PNG Minister for Education,one the author's brightest students.

[17] Fieldwork with Z. Kruczek, July 2006. See also Alpers (2005: 97).

high-powered weapons induces fear, bursts of mayhem, and the prolongation of vindictive activity (Pacific Islands Studies Program 1987: 97).

Matters reached extremes with the so-called 'Rambo' phenomenon among the Ipili Enga near Porgera between 2003 and 2012, which combined the traditional principles of payback killing (see Trompf 2021a: 31–40) with 'fetishization' of strong-armed protagonists in globalized popular culture (such as the comic-book hero 'The Phantom' (Beldi 2019)). Subsequent to wars in the 1980s (especially clashes between the Atakai and Apalaka tribes) that left subterranean scars, a terrible eruption occurred after the killing of two men. Significantly, one of them was one Ezekiel, who had achieved director-ship of the Ipila Porgera Investments Company, and had purportedly

Figure 6 Traditionally armed, an Ipili man stands sentinel outside his hamlet gate (also a bus stop on the highway) shortly after enemy raiders burnt down a neighbouring hamlet opposite, near Porgera mine, Engan highlands, PNG

Source: Photograph by the author, 2006.

embezzled money and distributed it to his own tribal lines. The killings were in broad daylight, brazen in the old style of the *peyapeya*, daring warriors who would unpredictably sidle up to an enemy and slit their throat. The immediate response to the outrages was to create a lethal equivalent in the form of a 'Rambo' (an idea taken from films and symbolizing a 'fighter for justice'), with embezzled money being used to purchase a quick-firing M16 on the black market. This weapon was taken to Ezekiel's grave to 'call his spirit' into it (*ge mini*); in his defenders' understanding, the new gun would keep magically 'eating everything' in its path like a goat. Before long the young man (or Rambo) possessing it was on a revenge rampage; but shortly so were other Rambos, armed comparably by tribes in need of defence and action. Most shot each other in action, buried in special heroes' graves iconically marked with pump-action guns; by 2012, 'one hundred men were killed, hundreds displaced, and nearly every structure in the area', churches and schools included, 'were destroyed and burned to the ground'. The few leaders left were liable for unaffordable compensation payments, and faced an inflated price on pigs and a fear that 'it will all start again'; only the SDA leadership remained intact, Adventists never having to fulfil reciprocal obligations with pigs and managing to get away during outbursts. The 'dark anthropology' necessary to report this pathological profile objectively surely points beyond the limitations of such study to address the problems it reveals; in this context, it screams to be supplemented by social healing (Jacka 2019: 43–50).

2.4.4 Sorcery and Witchcraft

Where do *sorcery and witchcraft* fit into all this? As noted before, while some researchers might concede the possibility of 'invisible violence', sorcery or witchcraft are difficult to place in this study except for when they involve physically harmful action against persons. As previously intimated (companion Element (Trompf 2021a, 2.1.1.6)), sorcery has been one trigger for armed feuding across the Pacific, and greater numbers of sorcery accusations enhance the likelihood of conflict (especially after the impact of new diseases), so the implications of inimical spiritual acts have clearly had the potential to generate violent reprisals. In the course of time across the wider Pacific, fear of ghosts overtook fear of sorcery (though of course the former could be manipulated to bring troubled relations) (e.g., Mitchell 1975: 87–101;

Westervelt (1915) 1985 (otherwise with caution)). Through Melanesia, however, sorcery and witchcraft in general belief and the practice of recognized specialists persist as matters of national concern. During colonial days, Melanesia's three most notorious forms of assault sorcery (*vada*, *sanguma*, and *vele*) spread after contact, the first especially along the east Papuan coast as far as Dobu, the second up the Sepik and Ramu rivers, and the third from the Russell Islands north to Malaita and easily eastwards to Guadalcanal, and they added to rising levels of anxiety over spiritual attack (Trompf 2021b: with Riebe 1987: 214 (PNG highland Kalam); Ivens (1927) 2018 (Malaita)). It was in a parallel context (and particularly in the 1890s) on the middle Ramu river (hinterland Madang) that the Rawa experienced heightened sorcery accusations, after increased instances of new sicknesses led to more armed conflict than 'in old times'. The German plantation economy reverberated inland, affecting land availability, trade, and thus group relations; indeed wherever colonial impacts intensified, the more the companionship of sorcery and homicide incidents (replacing war) manifested (Dalton 2000).

New and ever-pressing impulsions were placed on Islanders to adjust and 'improve life' in Melanesia. They were pressured to stop their fighting and 'objectionable' customs; relinquish houselines for substantial villages and move from inaccessibile areas; intermarry with previously antagonistic groups; accept supra-tribal government; practise universal religion; keep to government restrictions (in colonial days, these concerned liquor and race segregation); engage in business, cash-cropping, or other new economic possibilities; and acquire new goods. Following these pressures, a lurking fear came into play about a menacing inextinguishable-looking spectre from the unpacified past. This is the sense of sorcery or witchcraft as the 'enemy within' (cf. Middleton and Winter 1963: 77–110), which has steadily intensified because what is 'in' has become an enlarged 'field' on top of 'the enemy without' (not only old external enemies, but also potential new ones after flare-ups in widening arenas of contact), with any agent of inimical magic able to get closer to one's habitation through road-building or some hidden lure in a big village. Naturally, right from the start of native co-operation with expatriates, taking a role outside one's hamlet meant laying oneself open to being killed by sorcerers (and accepting recruitment for patrol by a colonial official could mean going right into enemy country!)

(Williams 1941: 88–9). Under steadily changing circumstances, formerly tolerated sorcerer/witch figures become conceived as worryingly 'non-reciprocal' rather than as valued protectors, as eerie isolates once-removed from communities that had hoped for a 'newly normalized' *pax* (Trompf 1997: 135). Rumours fly around, and those under threat call for support, whether over trouble, sickness, or death. In the ongoing transitional complexities, the more collective energies have been put into making and testing accusations of evildoing – with failed divination techniques sometimes producing an outrage – the more violence has had a chance to hold on (see Giay 1998: 60–3 on Paniai Lakes, West Papuan highlands), while the more sorcery self-legitimizes as the last-standing indigenous institution of local justice, the more likely it will be able to incite revenge killings (e.g., Maschio 1994: 196–7 on the Rauto, New Britain).

Thus it has to be admitted that the erosion of old arrangements by novel and more feared forms of sorcery (from near-contact into colonial times) has had implications for the history of Pacific Islander violence. In intriguing pockets where the resilience of custom shows even to this day, we still find indicators of the whole shift. The stubborn Kwaio traditionalists in Malaita's mountains accept that a great deal of 'foreign' sorcery knowledge and techniques, and accompanying spirit acquisitions, have been slowly creeping into their midst even from pre-contact days. These came first through trade exchanges with neighbours, and were then imported during nineteenth-century *kanak* labour-recruiting days. Later, these were followed by the purchase of 'modern commodities' for 'antisocial purposes', their use 'motivated by jealousy' against 'legitimately successful individuals within the Kwaio socioeconomic system'. However, their use also involved adopting techniques commonly found through the independent Solomon Islands as a method of curbing ambitions in those much more radically changed cultures, with 'sorcery-poisoning' of food included in this repertoire (Akin 1996: 158–9). The 'bleak picture' of sorcery as a canker of fear across the board in Melanesia points to new issues of psychosocial pathology that remain to be addressed (Stewart and Strathern 2018: 18; Bever 2000).

We should not forget how new types of sorcery were injected into warfare in places where that warfare continued longest. Postwar missionaries among the New Guinea highland Melpa rightly sensed that, in the fairly recent past, trade routes from the east had brought talk and practices of *kum(o)*, a form of witchcraft/sorcery that threatened intra-clan well-being (Strauss and Tischner (1962) 1990: 232–4). The near-neighbouring Wahgi had actually developed a ritual technique to handle its effects in war. If the dangerous bundle of an enemy *kum*-worker (*kum^{e}yi*) was detected near any hamlet, it could be redeployed: warriors jointly poked spears into it before battle, and any known associates of the *kum^{e}yi* on the battlefield would be selected for an agonizing death. As for witchcraft, Wahgi women were alleged to work *kum* by using their capacity to hold dangerous reptiles within their privates. In 1976, for a case taking place in the context of rapid social change, a man and a woman were jailed after admitting such harm-dealing, the woman confessing to having projected a snake from between her legs in the path of a truck; the snake's head having flicked up to hit the driver on the head, so that he fell ill with dysentery and later died in hospital. She had paid 200 kina towards purchasing that truck, yet the driver had refused to give her a lift home and retribution seemed deserved (Trompf 2008a: 63, 358; 2021, with Reay 1987: 92, 111).[18]

Later pressures of economic development (new businesses, transportation of cargoes along the PNG Highlands Highway) brought curious modifications to these practices; developments on the coasts had inevitable repercussions inland, and highly feared coastal sorceries (mostly going

---

[18] For comparable Polynesian beliefs that the most lethal (poisoning) sorcery disseminated across islands (but by god-effected anger) during post-contact times (1810s), see Kamakau 1991: 134–5 on Hawaiian *akua kumuhaka*. In wider Oceania the concept of 'sorcery spreading' still made sense, as evil borne from afar, and in Polynesia a return to witchcraft is seen as a calling up of the dead (or the Devil) to harm others, for example Anon. 2012; cf. 1 Sam. 28. On the 'twisted' appeal to Judas to justify sorcery in Melanesia, note McIntosh 1983: 231 (Eastern Elema). In Micronesia, of interest are Ponape memories of projecting 'phantom/ghost' armies in wars between tribes (1850) and against the Spanish (1890): Hanlon 1990: 110–17.

under the name *sanguma*) were used both to protect coastal workers in the mountains and add to the highlands' mix of recourses. Among the southern highland Mendi, so-called *botol* sorcery became a specialism of young men to rectify the arrogant overriding of traditional reciprocal obligations by those who were selfish with *bisnis* profits; glass splinters were secreted into their tinned meat (instead of the bamboo splinters that had been used in former times) Nihill 2001). In a reflection of sorcery's uncanny adaptability to changing circumstances, handling lethal potions called for innovative rituals. For the Wahgi, anybody carrying *kong-* ('killer'-) poison to sell for cash will have to throw stones across any river before they cross it (to avoid their own death), even though they are in a car and the poison is *bateri*, a lethal concoction made with battery fluid (Trompf 2008a: 368). Needless to say, modern pharmaceutical mixtures have now come into the picture, and are used in modern politics. Mixtures held in rubber mini-bottles at the chests of ambitious candidates can be quickly squeezed along a plastic tube and down their shirtsleeves into a rival's drink – appropriately, since a well-established Tok Pisin word for sorcery is *posin*.

Traditionally, with sorcery almost ubiquitously deployed against enemies for clan security, it was directed 'at random' against enemies unless the in-group of warriors encouraged the identification of specific targets (Ryan 1982: 2; with Patterson 1974: 156–60), but with the newer mixing of people, artful moves against individuals by paid functionaries have become more prevalent. Paradoxically, where sorcerers had previously played a 'domestic' role, punishing at their leaders' behests, now the former gained in standing and wealth. Pacification had decreased the authority of fight-leaders and chiefs with the coming of a new officialdom of law and order, reconfiguring the sorcerer within and between cultures as a singular anomaly or 'loose cannon'. Among the Mekeo, for a litmus test (Trompf 2008a: 76–8, 359–60), chiefs needed the *ungaunga* more than ever to offset their own social weakening, but the sorcerer was steadily released to exert his own power, with money-rich resentful individuals or families ready to pay him independently to work on their side in intra- as much as extra-village broils, and not unexpectedly – within the great social transformations of warrior cultures the world round – individual wielders of spiritual harm-dealing remain the longest-lasting and most adaptable protagonists for 'old cultural residues' (see Zelenietz and Lindenbaum 1981). Indeed, in recent surveys, in New Britain where the *Pax Germanica* had been so effectively stringent, and on Bougainville where prolonged fighting with modern weapons influences group memory, some respondents claimed sorcery, not tribal war, should be the traditional means of securing revenge (Zelenietz 1979; Forsyth 2019). This only underscores the value of diachronic approaches to ethnologic research: today, traps await young players who land in on a village sorcery situation and presume it is traditional in their snapshot ethnography, when contextualization and the plotting of change are essential for a mature comprehension.

As the 'dark anthropology' of gun violence currently puts pressure on academic researchers (indeed anthropologists) to do something to heal social problems, distressing scenarios connected to sorcery fears and accusations have increasingly drawn out of social scientists a humane concern, inspired by the need of the local community they study to remedy its pathology, which indeed leads them to be on the lookout for the best resources that can help that community handle newer stresses (Knauft 2019; cf. Forsyth and Eves 2015; Eves 2000). The disdain of anthropology's involvement in therapy becomes absurd, for even at the minimum recommendations may be made about inadequate healthcare in these communities, because the impoverishment of health specialists and services in the south-west Pacific is currently severe; thus, there are increased tendencies and opportunities to read sickness and death along traditional lines.

Our diachronic exploration now brings us to the present situation, in which emergent Melanesian nations and would-be autonomies are faced with the question of what to do with sorcery and witchcraft in the new millennium. In 1971, PNG parliamentary legislation prohibited sorcery as socially unacceptable, a decision that was in line with previous colonial impositions (note Gore 1965), but by 2013, the government had amended this ruling and instead treated homicides justified by alleged sorcery or witchcraft as part of the Criminal Code and deserving of the death penalty (Auka et al. 2015: 242–51). A generation or so ago, anything like the anti-sorcerer/witch 'drives' seen in Africa seemed to be absent (Trompf 2008a: 236; Federici 2009), and there was relative balance between those lamenting the presence of special harm dealers in society or wanting to bolster legal artifices against them (Baro 1973; Sillitoe

2000: 233–4), and those allowing them some social legitimacy, potentially as a 'great equalizer' or 'safety valve' (Sack 1974: 402; Belshaw 1955: 6; Spenger 2008). At the present time the trend is tipping is towards negativity: sorcery carries an implication of adding to unwanted violence because rumours can abound and be spread unrestrainedly, accusations of its practice are flung around, far outnumbering real cases (Stewart and Strathern 2004: 113–39), and provocative divination procedures are flaunted in already volatile situations: one of these is *pulim mambu*, in which a group loosely holds on to a 'deceased-directed' bamboo pole which points towards the culprit of a crime or misdemeanour (a technique that travelled over time from the New Guinea islands to the highlands) (Trompf 2021b: 315; cf. Schwarz 2011).

And for a minority of cultures and situations, the fear of witches, usually female, poses a newer threat (see Poole 1981: 58–76; Bercovitch 1989: 122–59; Zocca 2009). Accusations of witchcraft most often turn up in the PNG highlands within the context of continuing local and interregional rivalries (including religious conflict), and *violent outbursts against witches* – who are often accused of having ritually eaten the dead – have steeply risen there; such killings have only exacerbated inter-group homicides, which now often involve guns. Whereas there is greater fear of taking on male spirit-wielders, witches are mostly vulnerable women. In the past, though, their detection did not typically result in execution. Among the Wahgi, for instance, if a husband (allegedly) spotted a reptile or bat issuing from his wife's privates in the night, it would be a reason for divorce and to send her back to her people as a worker of *kum* too dangerous for his clan. This was basically exile, and if her home family would not reclaim her some needy marginal hamlets might risk welcoming her (Trompf 2018: 62–3). What we find all too commonly today are outbreaks of horrendous violence against women (and sometimes children) accused of witchcraft, in atrocities often carried out by young men not visibly supervised by elders.

In June 1986, to provide an example, a story was rapidly circulating in PNG's Chimbu Province that a young boy from the Sinasina district had died in the capital Port Moresby and that his death had been blamed on three girls from the Koge area, neighbouring Sinasina. When told about the accusations, significantly, one girl ran away and hanged herself; but the others were 'tied up and publicly tortured', and were mutilated while being ferociously questioned about their witchcraft (*kum*; Tok Pisin: *sanguma*). The Marist Father at Koge pleaded for the small crowd involved to desist, but they refused and the girls were then burnt alive. In other Chimbu cases around this time, certain older women's faces were smashed to a pulp on the claim they had killed a large number of people (*kilim planti manmeri*), and they were recognized as witches because their skin was 'greyish'. Young men played the role of executioners; when they were questioned by Brother Brendan Crowe (as Catholic Religious Education co-ordinator in the region), the killers implied they had been 'given free rein' by elders so that they could have their first taste of blood. While suspecting the women to be innocent, they believed they risked being killed themselves if they did not go through with the executions (Crowe 2008: 54–7).

Beyond the obscurity of such reportage came a growing plethora of PNG witch- and sorcerer-killing cases, mostly in highland areas (and among these mostly Chimbu, in rural, plantation, and urban contexts) but not exclusively so. Seventy-five instances were covered in the national press from March 2000 to December 2006; in most of these cases, the police did not intervene, or could not locate a body, or found identifying killers very difficult behind group solidarity; apparently, officers some-times accepted this practice of rough justice (for more on this topic, start with Urame 2008: 67–93; Gibbs 2012: 124–6). Torturing the suspected witches – using very hot wires, rods, or pokers – has been an all-too-common practice, because it is assumed that these women generally do not act alone and they are made to denounce their alleged co-workers; as a result, so the killing of small groups has frequently occurred, and occasionally children have been accused and despatched (esp. Bartle 2005: 238–40; Silas 1993: 67).[19] Those accused who escape will not last long near their accusers, and are forced to flee to Madang, Lae, or Port

---

[19] On recent incidents, Helen Davidson, 'Mass sorcery murder trial of more than 100 men begins in Papua New Guinea', *The Guardian*, 28 Mar. 2017, www.theguardian.com/world/2017/mar/28/mass-sorcery-trial-of-more-than-100-men-begins-in-papua-new-guinea; Helen Davidson, '"Bloodlust hysteria: Sorcery accusations a brutal death sentence in Papua New Guinea', The Guardian, 5 Jan. 2018, www.

Moresby; some of the unfortunate ones who have been caught have been cannibalized. In 2012, twenty-nine men were arrested for doing this in the Madang highlands, giving the traditional-sounding excuse that to consume occult powers secured their own 'invulnerablity' (*National* (PNG), 2 Jul. 2012).

2.4.5 Custodial Issues

As we bring our overview towards its conclusion, witch-killing raises *custodial questions*, especially to do with *gender* and the family and the *right of punishment* at different levels of society (from the family to the state, under so-called modernity). If we start from the PNG highlands – where gender inequality is most pronounced and warrior masculinity still actively expressed in the pockets of tribal warfare – and if we follow a giant bird's-eye view down to the coasts of the larger Melanesian islands and then out to the wider Pacific, as far as Polynesia's Marquesas – where noble women dominated the traditional priesthood and are now, in the outer islands, nearest to being the only female Catholic priests anywhere – the prevailing picture is of male dominance over family life (usually over extended families; cf., e.g., Macintyre and Spark 2017; Mantovani 1992; Howard and Kirkpatrick (1989) 2019: esp. 92–6; with Stacey 2011 on the outer Marquesas). Exceptions abound everywhere, of course. Even a Chimbu woman accused of witchcraft might possibly save her skin by persuading her people that her swift-flying powers could be put to the service of the clan into which she has married (not an impossibility traditionally, since there are female religious specialists) (Hughes 1985: 452–4; cf. Kyakas and Wiessner 1992 on Enga). And if PNG highland women of old might rise in prestige by supporting their husbands in inter-group relationships, today they can rise to national prominence as business-women and political leaders (e.g., Julie Akeke), organizers of women's associations (the Church-connected founders of the anti-drink Wok Meri, 'Women's Work'), theologians (like Rose Ninkama), and peacemakers (such as Josephine Be'Soer). The transmission of Christian and new civic

theguardian.com/world/2018/jan/05/bloodlust-hysteria-sorcery-accusations-a-bru tal-death-sentence-in-png, and so on.

and internationalized human values and the provision of education and new job opportunities have helped bridge the gender-inequality gap across the whole Pacific

Of course one can be cynical about the missionaries' 'sewing-machine model' of training women for home care, which projected a Western bourgeois ideal of dutiful, submissive womanhood on to the indigenous Pacific (note Jolly and MacIntyre 2010). In the author's experience at the grassroots, though, this has translated into strong female expressions of a community's hospitality, warm friendliness, and the gift-giving of handicrafts between otherwise mutually suspicious groups in an effort at unity through Church life.[20] Still, there hangs around the Pacific (as elsewhere!) the residual, ponderously ancient sense of right (Germ. *Recht*) that men are basically superior to women, who need controlling and disciplining in case they become too assertive, indeed dangerous, for men's interests. Across the Pacific, we must remind ourselves, gender relations vary, and in hierarchical societies, such as in Polynesia, noble women can reach the pinnacle of rule, as with Hawai'i's last sovereign Lili'okalani and Tonga's longest-serving monarch Queen Sâlote. Yet, unfortunately, we are committed to a book about violence, and the vulnerability of women in a 'once-were-warriors' world, in which the outlet of repressed masculine aggression can readily deflect back on wives, women, and children, is a serious Pacific-wide problematic. Male physical outbursts can be affected by a multitude of post-contact 'contributing factors', such as the overconsumption of alcohol (a by-now-perennial problem, noticeably during the coffee-selling season in the PNG highlands); gaming losses; insecure employment away from one's place of origin; perceived loss of freedom and self-worth in colonial contexts (as in French Polynesia); isolation under the threat of island inundation (atoll Micronesia); and post-traumatic stress after returning from war (e.g., from Bougainville in the 1990s). (For guidance, see Toft

---

[20] Also deferring to pioneer PNG gender studies researchers, including the author's student Louise Aitsi (with E. Cox in Tongamoa 1988: 22–37), and to the late Dr Anne Kaniku, the author's successor as Head, History Department, UPNG. See also Putt and Dinnen 2020.

and Bonnell 1985; Bradley 2001; Ellsberg et al. 2012; Jolly et al. 2012; cf. inter alia Marshall 1982; Dinnen 1999: 65–6; Jewkes et al. 2017.)

Rape, which can of course be inflicted on spouses (as well as on children and other males) is a form of male violence with a complex variety of motivations, including sexual frustration (especially in single males with jobs away from home in plantations and towns); jealousy and conflict over faithfulness and possessiveness; the effects of the sensuous civilization (*outré* suggestive advertising, pornography, cinematized sexual intercourse, 'sexting', etc.); and collective gang initiation, let alone prohibition of polygyny. A rape in a modern context can be evaded by the woman's indicating signs of menstruation, lactation, or vaginal discharge: the entrenched Pacific Islander male fear of female bodily fluids as dangerously polluting remains endemic. Traditionally, enemy women who had been ambushed would be raped despite such fears – if not killed – on the presumption that females with periods, during and after childbirth, those with any genital flux or those in preparation for marriage would be housed in seclusion by their 'sisters'. In the wake of rapid social change, however (such as the advent of sanitary pads, nursing bras, etc.), if a would-be sexual violator finds he is faced with 'pollution dangers', he may now be incited into plain and angrier physical violence.

Many memories of relevance flash before the author's mind here. Going back to mountainous PNG, various fieldwork experiences there with highlanders have struck me permanently. My research assistant from among the Bena Bena (PNG Eastern Highlands) suddenly confessed he was after a second wife because, in the case of his first, 'susu i slak tumas' (her breasts are now pendulous), and his purport was that he would easily make her second-rate. On another occasion, I attended a showing of *Gone with the Wind* at the local Goroka cinema (Eastern Highlands), to discover that many holes from hurled rocks had punctured the screen, thrown by the audience in outrage at what they perceived to be Scarlett O'Hara's increasingly grating attitude. I noted the glee in the eye when another of my research assistants (Mumeng, Morobe highlands), who admittedly was a recently reformed gang leader, brought his photographs of depressed grass where men had had 'Two Kina Meris', that is, women prostituted by their husbands to raise meagre family incomes by having sex with others. In

Banz (Wahgi country again), a Catholic nun presented me with a box of condoms, saying, 'Here, Garry, you take these, because no one else will use them here', explaining how women's health had plummeted due to the HIV/AIDS epidemic, with single male plantation workers wanting sex and local husbands prepared to send their wives off to wayside brothels to earn some extra cash. In a Port Moresby suburb, I was the stunned witness, along with others, of a strong young husband brazenly beating and slapping his wife all the way from the market to the shopfronts for not being where he had told her she was supposed to be. In lectures at the University of PNG, I also recall, young Enga men would exit the hall immediately and permanently if they smelt a female student with 'smelling rags' near their seats, and highlanders en bloc staged a walkout when a daring Trobriander student (the young Mrs Kasapwalova) gave the first indigenous defence of feminism in the main lecture hall (in 1972). These are key hints as to the general ethos in which most Melanesian women 'live and move and have their being', and within that ethos, their chances of suffering violent assault, particularly in PNG, are rising and becoming more noticeable. Women make too easy a target in ongoing or debased tribal conflict led by gun-owning 'warlords', and newly appointed PNG Prime Minister James Marape had to face the fact that 'the worst payback killing in our country's history' had occurred in July 2019, when in his very own Hela province, twenty-three women (two of them pregnant) and nine children were gunned down in an utterly unequal reprisal for the death of a tribal leader's mother (*Guardian*, 15 Jul. 2019).

Statistics are inadequate, but in some estimates as many as 70 per cent of women in PNG today either have been or will be raped at some time in their lives (including domestic rape, and traditional raiding, gang or multiple-perpetrator acts, witch-hunting, etc.). In a 2021 survey of ninety-five PNG women, almost half admitted their husbands had 'forced them to have sex', and whereas it would be reasonable to say that most criminal rape outside marriage contexts will be enacted by parties wilfully rejecting Christian injunctions, it is far from clear that this is true of intercourse imposed by male strength on wives, using claims to the right of access and domination in the 'marriage bed' that mix custom with biblical pronouncements about wives being 'subject to the [family] head' (Ephes. 5:24, yet cf. 33; with

Bainton et al. 2021).[21] Under-reporting of rape prevails in Melanesia, and also the whole Pacific, because of dread of the shame that befalls victims (cf. Epstein 1992: 228–30); the fact that the known 'spoiling' of a virgin can badly affect their marriage prospects; and lodging complaints about 'domestic-violence rape' casts a shadow over extended families. Rape within a household is probably the main reason why Melanesian (indeed most Pacific) legal systems find it awkward to criminalize domestic violence at all. But growing death tolls of women as a result of domestic violence are causing outlooks to shift; indeed, how has it come to such a state of affairs that domestic violence means that women would feel 'happier' to have AIDS, because being cared for with it amounts to 'freedom from marital conflict and subordination'? (Whiting and Harriman 2019; Wardlow 2019: 63; the quotation comes from a woman who was being sheltered by a plantation landowner). The Pacific independent nations, in claiming to embrace Christian and the noblest traditional standards – nations which typically invoke God in their constitutions and thus view Him as being behind their legal principles – have a duty of care for the lives and welfare of their citizens, and yet are faced with the haunting spectre of guilt for this violation of basic justice at an elevated national level (see, looking wider than the PNG context, Jolly et al. 2012; Biersack et al. 2017; Biersack and Mcintyre 2017; with Counts 1990; Anderson 2015; Hanlon 1998: 150–7).

In all this, questions of family life more generally and the custodianship of children invite discussion. Traditionally, marriages were made through inter-group exchanges, with a lot of preparatory arrangements and rules of residence after marriage; yet now (as has been exemplified on Rotuma) influences of 'the money system' mean the ceremonial aspects of this are often 'condensed to a bare minimum', and a symptomatic desacralizing 'showmanship' (wedding

---

[21] Consider summaries in Smith 2018: vol. 1, 242; and Mizumura 2011: vol. 2, 1204. In newsprint, see especially *The Telegraph* (UK), 21 Apr. 2013, for US academic B. Henderson on gang rape; *National*, 25 May 2021 on H. Joku on delaying rape trials. On violence against LGBTI Pacific persons, enforcing 'compulsory heterosexuality', see Besnier and Alexeyeff 2014. Any clerical sexual abuse by Indigenous islander perpetrators is a topic that is only now being opened for discussion.

dress, cake, high payoffs to relatives, departures from the 'proper way') have made the least violent contemporary Pacific societies susceptible to physical outbursts (Malo 1975: 28–31). Regarding upbringing, protective adoption by Islanders is a strong practice, though not unproblematic: on Palau, orphans remain depreciated and single or widowed fathers are pressed to relinquish their children (Barnett 1953: 383). In the absence of conflicts or emergencies that would require them to play their part as warriors, male youths are less supervised than formerly and make up their own rules within new official institutions (bullying, coercions of youngsters, degrading hazing, etc.). Undergraduate gangs, both offensive and defensive, wrecked the reputation of the University of PNG (Trompf 2000: 49; MacWilliam 2012: 134) while Christian-founded tertiary institutions gain respect as safe places, even if in some bodies affected by indigenous preconceptions – the theological college at Piula, West Samoa, for one – older candidates will physically buffet freshers into an appropriate silence, like uninitiated novices of old (cf. Tomlinson 2020: 24–5, 76–9). In rural areas, pressures from monetization (with 'loss of tradition, unemployment, changing social roles') have also affected the supervision of children, which non-nuclearized families can better sustain. A turn-of-millennium study of the Bumbita Arapesh (rural Sepik region, PNG) showed a rise in the popular desire to break rules and 'act badly' (*naneh nama*) in adolescent groups (Leavitt 1998: 173, 176, 179). In urban contexts, as in stressed squatter settlements, supervision of 'rascal' delinquents can fall into the hands of criminalized adults, who may then instruct them in gang rape as a form of initiation rite (Trompf 2008a: 380–1).

Yes, the religious pressure to Christianize that has so long been associated with peace now meets – especially because of shocking social dislocation in Melanesia but also because global criminal activity and gun-running threatens the Pacific generally – collective opinions that the most heinous offences deserve *violent punishment*, namely, the death penalty. Historical incidences aside, only for two independent Pacific Island nations is this penalty legally available, Papua New Guinea (until now!) and Tonga; and we ought to acknowledge that, as a 'world first,' the precolonial Christian Kingdom of Tahiti abolished the death penalty in 1824. But Pacific political entities (including those under neocolonial powers) inherited and still use non-traditional jail systems; despite the prisons' being hoped-for places of reform and allowing chaplaincy work, these systems can beget more violence (whether by warders or between inmates) and perpetuate it when felons are released.[22] The Pacific has also been bequeathed police systems, and nowhere on earth have police been impervious to abuse of power, violent arrests, or the torturing of offenders (shooting them for ostensibly treatening behaviour always being possible) (Reed 2011). When states of emergency are invoked and soldiers sent in, their temptation to use powerful weapons can escalate conflict and bring about collateral damage (e.g., Bogg 1985). Other issues of incarceration have arisen. PNG and (Micronesian) Nauru have committed themselves to accepting responsibility to run Australia's offshore detention centres for 'illegal immigrants' (under UNHCR regulations these inmates are defined as asylum seekers), and by keeping these would-be refugees from fair and reasonably speedy processing, they have become complicit in crimes against humanity, whether by political co-responsibility or through brutality and psychological torture in daily detention practice (esp. Boochani 2018: xii–xiii; with *Guardian*, 15 Jan. 2020).

Other issues of sociopolitical responsibility, to do with Pacific Island leadership involvement in structural violence, irresponsible environmental policy, undemocratic power establishments, corruption, money laundering, appalling labour conditions, and so on, and variegation of grassroots protest reactions (e.g., against demolitions of squatter housing, and more recently against Covid vaccination), require another book.[23]

3 Reflections and Recommendations

In line with my previous Element (Trompf 2021a), I continue to admit subjective dismay at having to dwell on negativities, even while pointing up those religious and other collective positivities countering forms of violence

---

[22] Ponder the trans-island reach of the Oceania Regions of the International Chaplains' Association. Regarding the death penalty, note its return to (US) Guam, its application on Rapanui (under Chile), and its de facto use in Indonesia's West/Papua (with the disappearances of dissidents).

[23] For example May 2022: 155–60. Also, on where Christianity is used for establishment politics, esp. Tomlinson and McDougall 2012.

that have accompanied dramatic social change. This dilemma has impelled me even more to include more theoretical reflection than provided in the earlier volume, to clarify further my own methodological stances towards the religion/violence connections, and also to think practically about current issues (or at least help researchers negotiate challenging materials and raise issues about solving human problems).

By now it will be obvious from my various writings that I am the proponent of 'retributive logic' as a cultural universal; in other words, that I hold members and especially the key knowledge-bearers of traditional religions – of the discrete small-scale cultures or religio-linguistic complexes discussed in both my Elements – to possess distinctive, decipherable ways of making concessions and showing antipathy towards others. Their repertories of action reflect a collective mental accounting as to why they follow such ways and should do so, and how they explain their 'cosmos' and what 'happens' in it over time, in the light of expectations that living agencies (including spirit-beings and the living dead) will concede or rankle. The logic of retribution is a matrix or complex of action and thought that comes into play when 'deed (*der Tat*) and expressible thinking about it (*das Wort, Logos*)' interlink. This is another way of saying that (under 'almost all communicable cognitive circumstances'), everybody can give *reasons* for why they act aggressively (or not) if they have been asked (indeed often challenged) to account for what they have done (in an identified action); and everybody is capable of 'having their own mind' about the violent things that others do and how relational affairs around them alter because of those violent deeds (esp. Trompf 2004: 19–22, 51–74, 203–4; 2008a: 1–18). Any act might have been misdirected or misinterpreted, the reasons given in explanation may be faulty or self-exonerating, and we cannot expect of retributive logic an 'Oxbridge' logician's standards because many emotional factors, spur-of-the-moment thinking, and autochthonous or 'folk' codes of reasoning, and so on, will come into play. In any case, there are 'social logics' (kinship rules, hierarchical principles, inventories of material value, etc.) that hold up within their own received standards of meaning (esp. Godelier 1986; Godelier and Strathern 1991 (including P. Lemonnier)); and even the insane expose their own verbally decipherable 'logics' (Bateson 1972: 177–337). After two Elements overviewing relevant Islander beliefs and behaviour patterns, then, it behoves us to enquire where retributive or payback theory sits in relation to 'violence and religion'.[24]

Clearly, important dialectical questions about violence and religion spring tangentially from our framing of retributive logic. First, we need to ask once more, given the new body of evidence herewith surveyed, whether 'religion' and 'violence' depend on each other; and the answer can no longer be in the affirmative. When members of small-scale warrior societies continue to think and act for the security of their total way of being, then the mutual dependence we admitted for traditional Pacific religions still applies. But once a vast, multifaceted corpus of religiosity intrudes on the old diversity, especially in what goes under the term 'Christianity', the situation changes dramatically and the analysis faces a challenge. In coping with this, critical researchers will have to deal with religion, especially Christianities, more maturely and with finesse. We must set aside as facile and prejudicial the habits of scholars who need to read 'religion' as delusional (e.g., La Barre 1955: 164–5), or rate 'all religions down the ages', and noticeably big monotheisms that share their 'corrupt beginnings', as basically materialist, like any 'cargo cult' (Hitchens 2008: 18–42, 186–7). Apologists, too, for *either* secularity *or* religious truth in driving a steel wedge between anthropology and mission, or those who hold 'Christianity' and 'social science' to be operationally incompatible, likewise yield no 'reciprocal promise' (accepting Hiebert 1978). It is philosophically inadmissible to turn conceptual colligations into living agents ('religion *does* this or that' to generate violence, for instance) when abstractions do nothing, even if agents are conditioned by ideas and social fixtures (Trompf 2007), and also because to do so is privative methodologically,

---

[24] Note that by my definition, retributive logic does not exhaust all acts of violence (some non-rational) or forms of reciprocity, does not apply only to religion typically conceived, and does not prevent 'positive' and 'negative' reciprocity as such being researched for their own sakes and linked to retribution (Ahrens 1986: 34–8). It takes its true mental force only when action and mental states are grasped as integrated and ready to be analytically probed as a nexus (Trompf 1997: 64–5; 2005: 220–2).

inhibiting a full flowering of interdisciplinary research. To pretend, moreover, that the protagonists of the Christian message in the Pacific have
heightened levels of violence, basically abetting or compromising with
hostilities, just warps reality, after balancing the evidence of the Pacific
religious scene 'in all its aspects', and mustering as many academic dis-
ciplines as possible for the assessment (Trompf 1988; 2008a: xiv). If, after all
their peacemaking and efforts for new friendly social orders, opposition to
occult maleficence and to cruel customs such as infanticide, live burials, and
widow execution (Snow and Waine 1979: 17; Maschio 1994: 231), and so on,
matters turn out against evangelizers' best intentions, their faith will have
required of them to confess their failings, and any outside criticism will
often paradoxically reflect competing versions of the same body of high
ethical ideals anyway.

Apropos of social changes in the Pacific, in any case, religious transformations have leaned overwhelmingly in favour of a Christian turn, and
there prevails a broad acceptance that Christianization is preferable to
preserving or restoring pre-pacification patterns of local conflict. That
cannot let issues of axiology be wished away. The Christian story in the
Islands has not always been pretty, and any complicity in violence showing up in the record demands critical analysis, including entanglements
with victors in 'contact wars' that in traditional logic meant the triumph of
the most powerful deity (note, e.g., Rennie 1989 on Kiribati; Hiroa and
Buck 1950: 519 on the Māori; Gilson 1980: 33 on the Cook Islands). Out of
the mêlée of moral judgements, however, with 'mission-bashing', accusations that Westernization brings on 'erring acculturation' like cargo cults
(cf. Baal 1960), as well as mainline Church irritations over fundamental-
ism, Pentecostalism, revival groups, and homegrown independencies,
engaged research in Oceania cannot go on without recognizing
Christianity's centrality. Ethnologists and ethno-historians now need to
work back from congregational life to tradition (Tomasetti 1976; Barker
1990; Ryle 2010; Schram 2018; Tomlinson 2020). Pacific Christianities
have fast shed their foreignness; and scholars are beginning to appreciate
what the wider world can learn from their adventures of adjustment
(Trompf 2006: 21–7). Furthermore, whatever the blundering, and frequent lack of self-criticism, the Pacific Islander 'consensus ideal' prevails

that old violent ways were rightly put away and the resurgence of inimical contentions best eschewed, an ideal exerting a moral pressure on visitors, scholarly investigators included, to chime in with its earnest tenor. Pacific Islanders, understandably, do not prefer a relativistic or purely humanistic approach to the big issues of religious truth and inimical violence, since for them a value system dislodged from divine revelation does not put the kind of ultimate demand on them that has been necessary to change their whole orientation of life. They are not basking in a post-Christian world where they can see in religions, flattened out with apparently 'objectivizing' ease, 'a vast series of rescue operations and fields for exercise of the human imagination', as one well-known book in humanist anthropology has it (Firth 1996: 213). This much I have learnt from Oceania's peoples: there are stark issues at stake, struggles of the soul between the high goal of indomitable goodwill – worth dying for – and insatiable pressures of payback standards. The consequent tricky part is, though, is how to foster what 'abounds in wisdom' among hundreds of indigenous traditions once their violent energies subside, to avoid colourless and less culturally creative alternatives.

The complex intersections of religion and violence in the Pacific Islands constitute a saga still unfolding, and there are various problems remaining to be solved (taken as problems, mind you, because of received biblical truths about peaceable, non-infringing behaviour that have also been enshrined in international codes; Trompf 1989b). Since this Element is multidisciplinary in nature, it can only be expected that, for the Islands, I believe that any increases in incidences of violence require coalitions of expertise to check them. How helpful it is to possess cultural knowledge for explaining why violence is expressed this way or that, and how enlightening to have an ethno-historian to put matters in context, a sociologist to plot various stresses and strains exacerbating conflict, a legal specialist to know what laws apply, or a missiologist who knows how wholesome thoughts can be twisted. But on the ground what is needed are well-informed social workers, pastoral carers and ministers, advocates for victims and peace-builders, backed if necessary by well-trained police, all hopefully ready to learn from grassroots experience and local viewpoints. I see it as a matter of policy in government that government departments and Church institutions should train and employ troubleshooters who attempt to grapple with the multifaceted causes and nature of violence, for their country's better management. Religion as such, of course, may no longer be the *key* reason for violence in a vastly changed Pacific, and we could have probed instead a mass of 'secular oppressions' and inequities contingent aupon the Islands being absorbed into the modern 'world system'. At any rate, my findings still have broad implications in the lessons that Pacific religious ideals can offer in removing social inequities, and in how sincere religious 'talk', trusted before political rhetoric in combined traditional and Christian terms, can crystallize the broadest social solidarity (cf. Wassmann 1998).

Specific practical recommendations are hard to make, given Oceania's inordinate complexities. My detailing in this Element already belies my stress on contextuality. But I highlight the usefulness of policy studies, peace and conflict studies, and the history of ideas (consciousness and religions) as the best *interdisciplinary* fields of study for understanding religion and violence, and as the source of practical responses to disentangle any problematic relationship in the Islands and encourage a noble spirituality to bring a just and secure concord (Trompf 2008a: 457–60; and with Clark et al. 2017). I recommend the study of retributive logic in theory and observations of it in cultural practice as offering the best multidisciplinary framing, particularly for halting tribal war, lethal sorcery, and witch-killing. Anthropologists need to adjust their agendas to help with providing practical advice that will maximize social healing, and certainly remain strong against the enticements of development consultancies (Brutti 2001). I recommend a concerted co-operation between churches and government to use resources in an ecumenical and non-partisan fashion in tapping the 'artifices of peace' (Ter Harr 2005), putting the quest for preventive measures before severe punition (indeed abolishing the death penalty), and imaginatively devising mechanisms for restorative justice that fit local conditions (Dinnen et al. 2010: Larcom 2015: 112–42; cf. Turner 1990: 176). Where international injustice exists in Oceania, as in the issues of nuclear testing and its consequences, the effects of global warming from irresponsible wealthier states, and the oppressions of neocolonial control (as in West Papua), the governments of the Pacific and the region's councils of churches should exert a greater collaborative voice, displaying their religious lessons for a world forever in need, it seems, of repacification.

References

Abong, M. 2018. 'Metamophoses of Nagriamel'. In *Kago, Kastom and Kalja*, eds. M. Abong and M. Tabari, 59–84. Marseilles.

Adams, R. 1984. *In the Land of Strangers*. Canberra.

Ahrens, T. 1986. *Unterwegs nach der verlorenen Heimat*. Erlangen.

Akin, D. W. 1996. 'Local and Foreign Spirits in Kwaio, Solomon Islands'. In *Spirits in Culture, History, and Mind*, eds. J. Bageo and A. Howard, 147–71. New York.

　2013. *Colonialism, Maasina Ruke, and the Origins of Malaitan Kastom*. Honolulu.

Aldrich, R. and J. Connell. 1998. *The Last Colonies*. Cambridge.

Alpers, P. 2005. *Gun-Running in Papua New Guinea*. Geneva.

Anderson, E. 2015. 'Domestic Violence and Society's Response in the Cook Islands'. (Doctoral dissertation, University of Otago, Dunedin.)

Angas, G. F. 1866. *Polynesia*. London.

Anon. 2012. 'Revival of Witchcraft in Tonga Concerns Authorities'. *Pacific Islands Report*, 19 Nov. pireport.org.

Anon. 2014. 'School Violence Is a National Problem in PNG'. *PNG Education News*, 10 Apr. edu.pngfacts.com.

Anova-Ataba, A. 1985. *D'Ataï à l'indépendance*. Nouméa.

Astroth, A. 2019. *Mass Suicides on Saipan and Tinian, 1944*. Jefferson, NC.

Athens, J. S. 2009. 'The Rise of the Saudeleur: Dating the Nan Madol Chiefdom, Pohnpe'. In *Vastly Ingenious*, eds. A. Anderson et al., 191–208. Dunedin.

Auka, R. et al. 2015. 'Sorcery and Witchcraft-Related Killings in Papua New Guinea: The Criminal Justice Response'. In *Talking It Through*, eds. M. Forsyth and R. Eves, 241–54. Canberra.

Baal, J., van. 1960. 'Erring Acculturation'. *American Anthropologist* NS 62.1: 108–21.

Bainton, A. et al. (eds.). 2021. *Unequal Lives*. Canberra.

Barker, J. (ed.). 1990. *Christianity in Oceania*. New York.

Barker. J. (ed.). 2016. *The Anthropology of Morality in Melanesia and Beyond*. New York.

2019. 'Converts, Christians and Anthropologists'. *The Australian Journal of Anthropology* 30.3: 277–93.

Baro, E. (ed.) 1973. *The Problem of Sorcery and Other Essays*. Rabaul.

Barnett, H. G. 1953. *Innovation*. New York.

Bartle, N. 2005. *Death, Witchcraft and the Spirit World in the Highlands of Papuan New Guinea*. Goroka.

Bateson, G. 1972. *Steps to an Ecology of Mind*. New York.

Beaglehole, J. C. 1966. *The Exploration of the Pacific*. Stanford, CA.

Beldi, L. 2019. 'The Phantom is a Huge Phenomenon in Papua New Guinea and a Symbol of Tough Fighters'. *ABC News*, 19 April abc.net.au/news/2019–04–19.

Belich, J. 1982. 'The New Zealand Wars, 1845–1870'. (Doctoral dissertation, University of Oxford, Oxford.)

Belshaw, C. 1955. *In Search of Wealth*. Arlington, VA.

Bennett, J. 2002. 'Roots of Conflict in Solomon Islands'. *State, Society and Governance in Melanesia Discussion Paper* 5: 1–16.

Bérard, L.-T. (1854) 1978. *Récit*. In *Le mémorial calédonien*, vol. 1: *1774–1863*, eds. P. Godard et al., 232–49. Nouméa.

Bercovitch, E. 1989. 'Mortal Insights: Victim and Witch in Nalumin Imagination'. In *The Religious Imagination in Papua New Guinea*, eds. M. Stephen and G. Herdt, 122–59. New Brunswick, NJ.

Bergendorff, S. 1998. 'The Sky Came Down: Social Movements and Personhood in Mekeo Society'. *Oceania* 69.2: 116–31.

Besnier, N. and K. Alexeyeff (eds.). 2014. *Gender on the Edge*. Hong Kong.

Bever, E. 2000. 'Witchcraft Fears and Psychosocial Factors in Disease'. *The Journal of Interdisciplinary History* 30.4: 573–90.

Bieniek, J. and G. W. Trompf. 1997. 'Nation under Curfew: Guns, Papua New Guinea, and Bougainville'. *Current Affairs Bulletin* 73.6: 27–8.

Biersack, A. et al. (eds.). 2017. *Gender Violence and Human Rights: Seeking Justice in Fiji, Papua New Guinea and Vanuatu*. Canberra.

Biersack, A. and M. Mcintyre (eds.). 2017. *Emergent Masculinities in the Pacific*. New York.

Binney, J. 1984. 'Myth and Explanation in the Ringatū Tradition'. *Journal of the Polynesian Society* 93.4: 351–8.

  2019. *Encircled Lands: Te Urewera, 1820–1921*. Wellington.

Binney, J. et al. 1979. *Mihaia: The Prophet Rua Kenana*. Wellington.

Black, P. M. 2015. '"Green Gold"'. (Doctoral dissertation, Australian National University, Canberra.)

Blaskett, B. 1993. 'Resistance Movement as a Nationalist Force: A Brief History of the OPM'. In *Islands and Enclaves*, ed. G. W. Trompf, 317–25. Delhi.

Blumenthal, M. D. et al. 1975. *More about Justifying Violence*. Ann Arbor, MI.

Boelaars, J. and A. Vriens. 1986. *Mengantar Suku Suku Irian Kepada Kristus*. 2 vols. Jakarta.

Bogg, B. 1985. 'Ol soldia i kilim 27 Enga pipel'. *Wantok* 559 (23 Feb.): 1–2.

Bohane, B. 2013. *The Black Islands*. Port Vila.

Boochani, B. 2018. *No Friend but the Mountain*, trans. O. Tofighian with M. Mansoubi. Sydney.

Bradley, C. 2001. *Family and Sexual Violence in Papua New Guinea*. Port Moresby.

Braithwaite, J. 2010. *Anomie and Violence: Non-truth and Reconciliation in Indonesian Peacebuilding*. Canberra.

Braithwaite, J. et al. 2010a. *Reconciliation and Architectures of Commitment.* Canberra.

2010b. *Pillars and Shadows.* Canberra.

Brown, G. 1908. *George Brown, D. D., Pioneer Missionary and Explorer.* London.

Brutti, L. 2001. 'Where Anthropologists Fear to Tread: Notes and Queries on Anthropology and Consultancy'. *Social Analysis* 45.2: 94–107.

Bryant, J. 1925. *Coral Reefs and Cannibals.* London.

Burridge, K. 1991. *In the Way.* Vancouver.

Burton-Bradley, B. G. 1972. 'Human Sacrifice for Cargo'. *Medical Journal of Australia* 2: 668–70.

1977. 'Guilty or Not Guilty'. *Catalyst* 7: 38–49.

Campbell, I. C. 1989. *A History of the Pacific Islands.* Christchurch.

Campbell, M. 2016. 'Religion and Resistance in West Papua'. (Master's dissertation, University of Sydney., Sydney)

Carter, R. 2006. *In Search of the Lost.* Canterbury, New Zealand.

Chappell, D. A. 1997. *Double Ghosts.* Armonk, NY.

Clark, P. 1975. *'Hauhau': The Pai Marire Search for Maori Identity.* Auckland.

Clark, S. G. et al. 2017. 'Interdisciplinary Problem Framing for Sustainability'. *Journal of Sustainable Forestry* 36.5: 516–34.

Cohn, N. 1970. *The Pursuit of the Millennium.* New York.

Connell, J. 1987. *New Caledonia or Kanaky?* Canberra.

1993. 'Politics and Tradition in Melanesia'. In *Islands and Enclaves*, ed. G. W. Trompf, 101–44. Delhi.

Corris, P. 1973. *Passage, Port and Plantation.* Melbourne.

Counts, D. A. (ed.). 1990. *Domestic Violence in Oceania.* Laie, HI.

Cowan, J. 1923. *The New Zealand Wars*, vol. 2. Wellington.

Crocombe, R. 2008. *The South Pacific.* Suva.

Crocombe, R. and M. Crocombe (eds). 1994. *Polynesian Missions in Melanesia*. Suva.

Crowe, B. 2008. 'On Experiences of Local Responses to Sanguma, July, 1996'. In *Melanesian Religion and Christianity*, ed. G. W. Trompf, 54–7. Goroka.

Dalton, B. J. 1967. *War and Politics in New Zealand, 1855–1870*. Sydney.

Dalton, D. 2000. 'Cargo Cults and Discursive Madness'. *Oceania* 70.4: 345–61.

    2007. 'When Is it Moral to Be a Sorcerer?' In *The Anthropology of Morality in Melanesia*, ed. J. Barker, 39–55. Aldershot.

Denoon, D. et al. (eds). 2004. *The Cambridge History of Pacific Islanders*. Cambridge.

Derlon, B. 2008. 'Human Sacrifice and Cargo Cult in New Ireland'. In *The Changing South Pacific*, eds. S. Tcherkézoff and F. Douaire-Marsaudon, trans. N. Scott, 106–31. Canberra.

Desroche, H. 1979. *The Sociology of Hope*, trans. C. Martin-Sperry. London.

Dinnen, S. 1998. 'Urban Raskolism and Criminal Groups in Papua New Guinea'. In *Gangs and Youth Subcultures*, eds K. and C. Hazlehurst, 267–306. New York.

    1999. 'Violence and Governance in Melanesia'. *Pacific Economic Bulletin* 14.1: 63–73.

    2001. *Law and Order in a Weak State*. Honolulu.

    2009. 'The Crisis of State in Solomon Islands'. *Peace Review* 21.1: 70–8.

Dinnen, S. et al. (eds.). 2010 *A Kind of Mending: Restorative Justice*. Canberra.

Douglas, B. 1998. *Across the Great Divide*. New York.

    2001. 'Encounters with the Enemy?' *Comparative Studies in Society and History* 43.1: 37–64.

Dousset-Leenhardt, R. 1978. *Colonialisme et contradictions*. Paris.

Droogan, J., and L. Waldek. 2015. 'Continuing Drivers of Violence in Honiara'. *Australian Journal of International Affairs* 693: 285–304.

Earle, A. 1832. *Narrative of a Nine Months' Residence in New Zealand in 1827.* London.

Elbert, S. H., and T. Monberg (eds.). 1965. *From the Two Canoes.* Copenhagen.

Ellis, W. (1842) 1969. *Polynesian Researches.* Rutland, VT.

Ellsberg, M. et al. 2012 *Violence against Women in Melanesia.* Canberra.

Elsemore, B. 1985. *Like Them that Dream.* Tauranga.

Epstein, A. L. 1992 *In The Midst of Life.* Berkeley, CA.

Eri, V. 1973. *The Crocodile.* Harmondsworth.

Eves, R. 2000 'Sorcery's the Curse'. *Journal of the Royal Anthropological Institute* 6.3: 453–68.

Fairio, B. 1985. 'The Struggle for West Papua'. (Unpublished paper, UPNG, Port Moresby)

Fakamuria, K. et al. (1995) 'Futuna. Aniwa, Aneityum and Erromango'. In *Melanesian Politics*, ed. H. van Trease, 377–402. Canterbury, NZ.

Federici, S. 2009. 'Witch-Hunting, Globalization, and Feminist Solidarity in Africa Today'. *Wagadu* 6: 49–64.

Fergie, D. 1986. 'Prophecy and Leadership'. In *Prophets of Melanesia*, ed. G. W. Trompf, 89–104. Suva.

Field, M. et al. 2005. *Speight of Violence.* Auckland.

Filemoni-Tofaeono, J. A., and L. Johnson. 2006. *Reweaving the Relational Mat.* New York.

Firth, R. 1996. *Religion: A Humanistic Interpretation.* London.

Firth, S. 1983. *New Guinea under the Germans.* Melbourne.

(ed.) 2006. *Globalisation and Governance in the Pacific Islands.* Canberra.

Fischer, S. R. 2013. *A History of the Pacific Islands.* London.

Fitzroy, R., and C. Darwin. 1839. 'A Letter, Containing Remarks on the Moral State of Tahiti'. *South African Christian Recorder* 2.4: 221–7.

Flichler, P. et al. 1938. *The Arrow Flieth by Day*. Minneapolis.

Forman, C. W. 1982. *The Island Churches of the South Pacific*. Maryknoll, NY.

(ed.) 1992. *Island Churches*. Suva.

Forsyth, M. 2019. 'Kill All the Sorcerers'. *British Journal of Criminology* 59.4: 842–61.

Forsyth, M. and R. Eves (ed.). 2015. *Talking It Through*. Canberra.

Foucault, M. 1980. *Power/Knowledge*, ed. and trans. C. Gordon. New York.

Fraenkel, J. 2004. *The Manipulation of Custom*. Wellington.

Fraenkel, J., and S. Firth (eds.). 2007. *From Election to Coup in Fiji*. Canberra.

Freeman, J. D. 1959. 'The Joe Gimlet or Siovili Cult'. In *Anthropology in the South Seas*, eds J. D. Freeman and W. R. Geddes), 185–200. New Plymouth, NZ.

Gajdusek, D. C. 1967. *South Pacific Journal*. Bethesda, MD.

Gaisseau, P.-D. (dir.) 1961. *Le ciel et la boue* [Ardennes documentary film]. Paris.

García, F. (1683) 2004. *The Life and Martyrdom of the Venerable Father Diego Luis de San Vitores* (trans. M. M. Higgins et al.). Hagatña.

Garrett, J. 1982. *To Live among the Stars*. Geneva.

Gascoigne, J. 2014. 'Religion and Empire in the South Seas in the First Half of the Nineteenth Century'. In *The Routledge History of Western Empires*, eds R. Aldrich and K. McKenzie, 439–53. London.

Gesch, P. 1990. 'The Cultivation of Surprise and Excess'. In *Cargo Cults and Millenarian Movements*, ed. G. W. Trompf, 213–38. Berlin.

(ed.) 2009 *Mission and Violence*. Madang.

Giay, B. 1989. 'The Rebels and Cargoistic Ideas in Irian Jaya'. *Catalyst* 9.2: 131–46.

1998. *Gembelakanlah Umatku*. Jayapura.

Gibbs, P. 2012. 'Engendered Violence and Witch-Killing in Simbu'. In *Engendering Violence in Papua New Guinea*, eds M. Jolly et al.), 107–35. Canberra.

Gilson, R. 1980. *The Cook Islands, 1820–1950*, ed. R. Crocombe. Suva.

Godard, P. et al. 1978. *Mémorial Caledonien*, vol. 1: *1774–1863*. Nouméa.

Godelier, M. 1986. *The Mental and the Material*. London.

Godelier, M. and M. Strathern (eds.) 1991. *Great Men and Big Men*. Cambridge.

Gore, R. 1965. *Justice versus Sorcery*. Brisbane.

Gotman, K. 2018. *Choreomania*. Oxford.

Grainger, G. 1992. *Wainiqolo: Last Polynesian Warlord*. Sydney.

Greenwood, W. 1980. *The Upraised Hand*. Wellington.

Grimble, A. 1932. 'Religious Disturbances'. In *Gilbert and Ellice Colony Report for 1929–30*, 31–4. London.

   1952. *A Pattern of Islands*. London.

Guiart, J. 1951. 'Forerunners of Melanesian Nationalism'. *Oceania* 22.2: 81–90.

   1968. 'Le Cadre social traditionnel et la rébellion de 1878 dans le pay de La Foa, Nouvelle-Calédonie'. *Journal de la Société des Océanistes* 24.24: 97–119.

Gunn, W., and Mrs Gunn. 1924. *Heralds of the Dawn*. London.

Gunson, N. 1962. 'An Account of the Mamaia or Visionary Heresy of Tahiti, 1826–1841'. *Journal of the Polynesian Society* 71.2: 208–45.

   1969. 'Pomare II of Tahiti and Polynesian Imperialism'. *Journal of Pacific History* 4.1: 65–82.

Hamilton, S. 2016. *Stolen Island*. Wellington.

Hanlon, D. L. 1990. 'Sorcery, "Savage Memories", and the Edge of Commensurability for History in the Pacific'. In *Pacific Islands History*, ed. B. Lal, 107–28. Canberra.

   1998. *Remaking Micronesia*. Honolulu, HI.

2019. *Upon a Stone Altar*. Honolulu, HI.

Hannemann, E. F. 1948. 'Le Culte de Cargo en Nouvelle-Guinée'. *Le Monde non-chrétien* 8: 937–62.

Hassell, J. 2005. 'The Bahá'i Faith in the Pacific'. In *Vision and Reality in Pacific Religion*, eds. P. Herda, M. Reilly, and D. Hilliard, 266–86. Canterbury, NZ.

Havea, J. (ed.). 2017. *Postcolonial Voices from Downunder*. Eugene, OR.

Hedley, C. 1896. 'General Account of the Island of Funafuti'. *Australian Museum Publications* 3.2: 1–72.

Hemer, R. 2013. *Tracing the Melanesian Person*. Adelaide.

Hempenstall, P. 1978. *Pacific Islanders under German Rule*. Canberra.

Hempenstall, P., and N. Rutherford. 1984. *Protest and Power in the Colonial Pacific*. Suva.

Hermann, E. 1987. '"Nem bilong 'Kargo Kalt' em I Tambu Tru"'. (Master's dissertation, The University of Tübingen, Tübingen)

Hermkens, A.-K. 2013. 'Like Moses Who Led His People to the Promised Land'. *Oceania* 83.3: 193–206.

2015. 'Marian Movements and Secessionist Warfare in Bougainville'. *Nova Religio* 18.4: 35–54.

Hezel, F. 1971. 'The Spanish Capuchins in the Carolines'. *Micronesian Reporter* 18.2: 36–42.

Hiebert, P. G. (1978) 2002. 'Missions and Anthropology: A Love/Hate Relationship'. *Missiology* 6.2: 165–80.

Hiney, T. 2000. *On the Missionary Trail*. New York.

Hiroa, T. R., and P. Buck. 1950. *The Coming of the Maori*. Christchurch, NZ.

Hitchens, C. 2008. *God Is Not Great*. New York.

Hogbin, I. 1970. *Experiments in Civilization*. New York.

Hours, B. 1974. 'Un Mouvement politico-religieux néo-Hébridais'. *Cahiers ORSTOM* 11.51–2:207–31.

Howard, A., and J. Kirkpatrick. (1989) 2019. 'Socialization and Character Development'. In *Developments in Polynesian Ethnology*, eds. A. Howard and R. Borofsky, 92–6. Honolulu, HI.

Howley, P. 2002. *Burning Spears and Mending Hearts*. London.

Husserl, E. (1936) 1970. *The Crisis of the European Sciences*, trans. D. Carr. Evanston, IL.

Hughes, J. 1985. 'Chimbu Worlds: Experiences of Continuity and Change by a Papua New Guinea Highland People'. (Doctoral dissertation, LaTrobe University, Melbourne)

Hviding, E. 2011. 'Re-placing the State in the Solomon Islands'. In *Made in Oceania*, eds. E. Hviding and K. M. Rio, 51–89. Wantage.

IASER. 1978–9. *Post-Courier Selective Index*. 7 vols. Port Moresby

Inglis, A. 1974. *Not a White Woman Safe*. Canberra.

Ivens, W. G. (1927) 2018. *Revival*. New York.

Jacka, J. K. 2015. *Alchemy in the Rain Forest*. Durham, NC.
　　2019. 'Resource Conflicts and the Anthropology of the Dark and the Good in Highland Papua New Guinea'. *The Australian Journal of Anthropology* 30.1: 35–52.

James, C. R. 2002. 'From Village to City: Samoan Migration to California'. In *Pacific Diaspora*, eds. P. R. Spickard et al., 118–34. Honolulu, HI.

Jeffrey, R. (ed.) 2017. *Traditional Justice in Practice*. New York.

Jewkes, R. et al. (2017). 'Enduring Impact of Conflict on Mental Health and Gender-based Violence Perpetration in Bougainville'. *PLoS One* 12.10: 1–13 (online: journals.plos.org).

Jojoga Opeba, W. 1993. 'The Papuan Republican Fighters Army'. In *Islands and Enclaves*, ed. G. W. Trompf, 262–88. Delhi.

Jolly, M., and M. MacIntyre (eds.). 2010. *Family and Gender in the Pacific*. Cambridge.

Jolly, M., C. Stewart, with C. Brewer (eds.) 2012. *Engendering Violence in Papua New Guinea*. Canberra.

Kamakau, S. M. 1991. *Ka Poʻe Kahiko*, trans. M.K. Pukui, ed. D.B. Barrère). Honolulu, HI.

Kamma, F. C. 1972. *Koreri: Messianic Movements in the Biak-Numfor Area*. The Hague.

1977. *"Dit wonderlijk werk"*. Oegstgeest.

Kaplan, M. 1995. *Neither Cargo nor Cult*. Durham, NC.

Keesing, R. M. 1982. 'Traditionalist Enclaves in Melanesia'. In *Melanesia: Beyond Diversity*, eds. R. J. May and H. Nelson, vol. 1, 39–54. Canberra.

1995. 'Murder on Mount Austin'. In *Beyond Textuality*, eds. G. Bibeau and E. Corin, 209–29. Berlin.

Kemelfield, H. 1976. 'The Causes of the 1878 Insurrection in New Caledonia'. (Honours subthesis, UPNG, Port Moresby)

Kenilorea, Sir P. 2008. *Tell It as It Is*, ed. C. Moore. Taipei.

Kijne, I. 1993–4. 'Hai Tanak Ku Papua'. *West Papua Bulletin (PNG)*, 1–3: 2 (in each issue).

King, D. S. 2011. *Food for the Flames*. San Francisco.

King, J. 1899. *Christianity in Polynesia*. Sydney.

King, M. 2003. *The Penguin History of New Zealand*. Auckland.

Kituai, A. I. K. 1998. *My Gun, My Brother*. Honolulu, HI.

Knauft, B. 2019. *Good Life in Dark Times?* Special issue. *TAJA* 32: 3–17.

Kolshus, T., and E. Hovdhaugen. 2010. 'Reassessing the Death of the Bishop John Coleridge Patteson'. *Journal of Pacific History* 45.3: 331–55.

Kroef, J. M. van der. 1959. 'Culture Contact and Culture Conflict in Western New Guinea'. *Anthropological Quarterly* 32.3: 134–60.

Kruczek, Z. 2011. *A Short History of Christianity in Melanesian Countries*. Mount Hagen.

Kyakas, A., and P. Wiessner. 1992. *From Inside the Women's House*. Brisbane.

La Barre, W. 1955. *The Human Animal*. Evanston, IL.

Lal, B., and M. Pretes (eds.). 2008. *Coup*. Canberra.

Landes, R. 2011. *Heaven on Earth*. New York.

Laracy, H. (ed.) 1983. *Pacific Protest*. Suva.

Larcom, S. 2015. *Legal Dissonance*. Oxford.

Lattas, A. 1998. *Cultures of Secrecy*. Madison, WI.

Latukefu, S. 1974. *Church and State in Tonga*. Brisbane.

Lawrence, P. 1954. 'Cargo Cult and Religious Beliefs among the Garia'. *International Archives of Anthropology* 47.1: 1–20.

   1967. *Road Belong Cargo*. Melbourne.

Leavitt, S. C. 1998. 'The Bikhet Mystique: Masculine Identity and Patterns of Rebellion among Bumbita Adolescent Males'. In *Adolescence in Pacific Island Societies*, eds. G. Herdt and S. C. Leavitt, 173–194. Pittsburgh, PA.

Lee, H. M. 2003. *Tongans Overseas: Between Two Shores*. Honolulu, HI.
   2018. 'Becoming Tongan Today'. In *Change and Continuity in the Pacific*, eds. J. Connell and H. Lee, 118–35. New York.

   (ed.). 2019. *Pacific Youth: Local and Global Futures*. Canberra.

Loeliger, C. E. and G. W. Trompf (eds.). 1985. *New Religious Movements in Melanesia*. Suva.

Lohmann, R. I. 2014. 'A Cultural Mechanism to Sustain Peace: How the Asabano Made and Ended War', *Anthropologica* 52.2: 285–300.

Longgar, W. K. 2008. *Kaugu Gunan ma Kaugu Pia, My Villlage and My Land*. Goroka.

Loomis, T. M. 1984. 'The Counterfeit Savage (Te Aviri a te Etene): A Study of Cook Islands Migrants, Class and Racialization in New Zealand'. (Doctoral dissertation, University of Adelaide, Adelaide.)

Lovett, R. 1914. *James Chalmers*. London.

Lyall, A. C. 1979. *Whakatohea of Opotiki*. Wellington.

Macintyre, M. 1995. 'Violent Bodies and Vicious Exchanges'. *Social Analysis* 37: 29–43.

Macintyre, M., and C. Spark (eds.). 2017. *Transformations of Gender in Melanesia*. Canberra.

Macnaught, T. J. 1982. *The Fijian Colonial Experience*. Canberra.

MacWilliam, S. 2012. 'Crunch-time for the University of Papua New Guinea'. *Pacific Journalism Review* 20.2: 118–39.

Maiden, P. 2003. *Missionaries, Headhunters and Colonial Officers*. Brisbane.

Malinowski, B. 1945. *The Dynamics of Culture Change*. London.

Malo, T. 1875. *Rotuman Marriage*. Suva.

Mamak, A. et al. (eds.). 1979. *Race, Class and Rebellion in the South Pacific*. Sydney.

Mantovani, E. 1977. 'A Fundamental New Guinea Religion'. *Point* (special issue) 1: 154–65.

1992. *Marriage in Melanesia*. Goroka.

2021. *History of Yobai*. Ho Chi Minh City.

Marjen, C. 1967. 'Cargo Cult Movement–Biak'. *Journal of Papua and New Guinea Society* 1.2: 62–5.

Marshall, M. (ed.) 1982. *Through a Glass Darkly*. Port Moresby.

Mariner, W. (1817) 1991. *An Account of the Natives of the Tonga Islands*, ed. J. Martin (2 vols), vol. 1. Nuku'alofa.

Maschio, T. 1994. *To Remember the Faces of the Dead*. Madison, WI.

Mathew, P. K. 1996. 'Changing Trends in Tribal Fights in the Highlands of Papua New Guinea'. *Papua New Guinea Medical Journal* 39.2: 117–20.

Maude, H. E. 1973. 'The Raiatean Chief Auna and the Conversion of Hawaii'. *Journal of Pacific History* 8: 188–91.

Maxwell, D. 2005. 'Decolonization'. In *Missions and Empire*, ed. N. Etherington, 285–306. Oxford.

May, J. D. 2003. *Transcendence and Violence*. London.

May, R. J. (ed.). 1982. *Micronationalist Movements of Papua New Guinea*. Canberra.

2022. *State and Society in Papua New Guinea*. Adelaide.

May, R. J., and M. Spriggs (eds.). 1992 *The Bougainville Crisis*. Bathurst, NSW.

Mayo, J. 1973. 'A Punitive Expedition in British New Guinea'. *Journal of Pacific History* 8: 89–99.

McIntosh, A. 1983. 'Sorcery and Its Social Effects amongst the Elema of Papua New Guinea'. *Oceania* 53.3: 224–32.

McLaughlin, G. 2017. *A Short History of the New Zealand Wars*. Auckland.

McLean, A. 2014. 'Corporal Punishment of Children in Tonga'. *Asia Pacific Journal of Human Rights and the Law* 15.1–2: 73–118.

McSwain, R. 1979. *The Past and Future People*. Melbourne.

Meggitt, M. J. 1977. *Blood Is Their Argument*. Brisbane.

Meijl, T. van, and J. Miedema (eds.). 2004. *Shifting Images of Identity in the Pacific*. Leiden.

Métais, E. 1967. *La Sorcellerie canaque actuelle*. Paris.

1988. *Au Commencement était la terre*. Bordeaux.

Middleton, J., and E. Winter (eds.). 1963. *Witchcraft and Sorcery in East Africa*. London.

Mikaere, B. 1997. *Te Maiharoa and the Promised Land*. Auckland.

Miller, J. G. 1948. 'Naked Cults in Central West Santo'. *Journal of the Polynesian Society* 57: 331–2.

Misur, G. X. 1973. 'From Prophet Cult to Established Church'. In *Conflict and Compromise: Essays on the Maori since Colonisation*, ed. I. H. Kawharu), 95–115. Wellington.

Mitchell, R. E. 1975. 'Micronesian Ghosts and the Limits of Functional Analysis'. *Asian Folklore Studies* 34.2: 87–101.

Mizumura, A. 2011. 'Incidence of Rape'. In *Encyclopedia of Women in Today's World*, eds. M. Z. Stange et al., vol. 2, s.v. Washington.

Moore, C. 2004 *Happy Isles in Crisis*. Canberra.

2017. *Making Mala*. Canberra.

Mrgudovic, N. 2012. 'Evolving Approaches to Sovereignty in the French Pacific'. *Commonwealth and Comparative Politics* 50.4: 456–73.

Mühlmann, W. E. 1955 *Arioi und Mamaia*. Wiesbaden.

Munro, D. 1982. 'The Lagoon Islands: A History of Tuvalu 1820–1908'. (Doctoral dissertation, Macquarie University, Sydney)

Myrttinen, H. 2015. 'Under Two Flags: Encounters with Israel, *Merdeka* and the Promised Land in *Tanah Papua*'. In *From 'Stone Age' to 'Real Time'*, eds. M. Slama and J. Munro, 125–44. Canberra.

Naepels, M. 2017. *War and Other Means*. Canberra.

Narokobi, B. 1988. *Concept of Ownership in Melanesia*. Goroka.

Neilson, D. 2021. *A History of Christianity in West Papua to 2000*. Delhi.

Nevermann, H. 1968. 'Die Religionen der Südsee'. In *Die Religionen der Südsee und Australiens*, eds. H. Nevermann et al., 5–123. Berlin.

Newell, M. J. 1992. *Seraja Geraja di Indonesia*. Manokwari.

Newland, L. 2015. 'The Lost Tribes of Israel – the Genesis of Christianity in Fiji'. *Oceania* 85.3: 256–76.

Nihill, M. 2001. 'Botol Sorcery in the Southern Highlands of Papua New Guinea'. *Social Analysis* 45.1: 103–21.

Niukula, P. 1992. *The Three Pillars*. Suva.

O'Brien, F. 1922. *Atolls of the Sun*. London.

O'Callahan, M.-L. 1999. *Enemies Within*. Sydney.

Ogan, E. (1974). 'Cargoism and Politics in Bougainville 1962–1972'. *Journal of Pacific History* 9: 117–29.

Ondawame, J. O. 2003. 'The Colonial Politics of Papuan Rights in Historical Perspective'. In *Plight of Papua*, eds. J. Bieniek and G. W.Trompf, special issue of *Mi-cha-el* 9: 103–18.

2006. 'West Papua'. In *Cultural Genocide and Asian State Peripheries*, ed. B. Sautman, 103–38. New York.

Ortner, S. 2016. 'Dark Anthropology and Its Others: Theory Since the Eighties'. *HAU: Journal of Ethnographic Theory* 6.1: 47–73.

Overweel, A. (ed.). 1994. *Archives relating to Netherlands New Guinea History*. Leiden.

Pacific Islands Studies Program. 1987. *Wansalawara: Soundings in Melanesian History*. Honolulu, HI.

Paton, J. G. 1889. *An Autobiography*, ed. James Paton. New York.

Patterson, M. 1974. 'Sorcery and Witchcraft in Melanesia'. *Oceania* 45.2: 132–60.

Petersen, G. 1993. *Lost in Weeds*. Honolulu, HI.

    2014. 'The Possibilities of Violence and the Skills to Avoid it'. *Anthropologica* 56: 315–26.

Plate, C. 2005. *Restless Spirits*. Sydney.

Poole, F. J. P. 1981 'Tamam: Ideological and Sociological Configurations of Witchcraft among the Bimum-Kuskusman'. *Social Analysis* 8: 58–76.

Putt, J., and S. Dinnen. 2020. *Reporting, Investigating and Prosecuting Family and Sexual Violence Offences in Papua New Guinea*. Canberra.

Quanchi, M., and R. Adams (eds.). 1993. *Culture Contact in the Pacific*. Cambridge.

Ramesh, S. 2008. 'Reflections on the 1987 Fiji Coups'. *Fijian Studies* 5.1: 162–76.

    2010. 'History of Inter-Group Conflict and Violence in Modern Fiji'. (Master's dissertaton, University of Sydney)

Ramsted, M. 2003. *Conversion in the Pacific: Eastern Polynesia Latter-day Saints' Conversion Accounts*. Bergen.

Ratuva, S. 2013. *Politics of Preferential Development*. Canberra.

Reay, M. 1959. *The Kuma*. Melbourne.

    1987. 'The Magic-Religious Foundations of New Guinea Highlands Warfare'. In *Sorcerer and Witch in Melanesia*, ed. M. Stephen, 93–120. Melbourne.

Reed, A. 2011. 'Number One Enemy: Police Violence and the Location of Adversaries in a Papua New Guinea Prison'. *Oceania* 81.1: 22–35

Rello, R. (dir.) 2019. *The Cult of the Black Jesus* (Documentary film; YouTube.com).

Rennie, S. 1989. 'Missionaries and War Lords: A Study of Cultural Interaction on Abalang and Tarawa'. *Oceania* 60.2: 125–38.

Richardson, D. 1976. *Peace Child*. Glendale, CA.

Riebe, I. 1987. 'Kalam Witchcraft'. In *Sorcerer and Witch in Melanesia*, ed. M. Stephen, 211–45. Melbourne.

Rijksen, R. 1973. *Mission on Irian Jaya*. [Sumba?].

Robbins, J. 2004. *Becoming Sinners*. Berkeley, CA.

Robertson, R. T., and A. Tamanisau. 1988 *Fiji: Shattered Coups*. Sydney.

Robie, R. 1989. *Blood on Their Bones*. London.

Robin, R. W. 1980. 'Missionaries in Contemporary Melanesia'. *Journal de la Société des Océanistes* 69: 261–78.

Rodman, M., and M. Cooper (eds.). 1983. *The Pacification of Melanesia*. Lanham, MD.

Rosenberg, H. von. 1878. *Der malayische Archipel*. Leipzig.

Rosenfeld, J. 1999. *The Island Broken into Two Halves*. University Park, PN.

Ryan, D. 1982. 'The Making of a Sorcerer among the Toaripi of Papua New Guinea' (Unpublished paper delivered to the LaTrobe RCSWPS Conference, 20 May 1982, Melbourne).

Ryan, W. P. 1973. *Papua New Guinea, Department of the Chief Minister: Guide to Functions*. (Mimeographed regulations (pre-Independence)), Port Moresby.

Ryle, J. 2005. 'Roots of Land and Church: The Christian State Debate in Fiji'. *International Journal for the Study of the Christian Church* 5.1: 58–78.

2010. *My God, My Land*. New York.

Sack, P. 1974. 'Crime or Punishment: The Role of the Sorcerer in Traditional Tolai Law'. *Anthropos* 69.3–4: 402

2001. *Phantom History*. Canberra, 2 vols.

Salisbury, R. F. 1958. 'An Indigenous New Guinea Cult'. *Kroeber Anthropological Society Papers* 18: 67–78.

Sarei, A. H. 1974. *Traditional Marriage and the Impact of Christianity on the Solos of Buka Island*. Port Moresby.

Saunana, J. 1980. *The Alternative*. Honiara.

Saussol, A. 1979. *L'Héritage*. Paris.

Sayers, G. F. 1930. *Handbook of Tanganyika*. London.

Scarr, D. 1976. 'Cakobau and Ma'afu: Contenders for Preeminence in Fiji'. In *Pacific Islands Portraits*, eds. J. W. Davidson and D. Scarr, 95–126. Canberra.

Schiefenhövel, W. 2009. 'Explaining the Inexplicable: Traditional and Syncretistic Religiosity in Melanesia'. In *The Frontiers Collection*, eds E. Voland and W. Schiefenhövel, 143–64. New York.

Schieffelin, E. L. 1981. 'The End of Traditional Dance, Music and Body Decoration in Bosavi, Papua New Guinea'. In *The Plight of the Peripheral People of Papua New Guinea*, vol. 1: *The Inland Situation*, ed. R. Gordon, 1–22. Cambridge, MA.

Schlesier E. 1953. *Die Erscheinungsformen des Männerhauses und das Klubwesen in Mikronesien*. The Hague.

Schmitz, C. A. (1960). *Historische Probleme in Nordost-Neuguine*. Wiesbaden.

Schram, R. 2018. *Harvests, Feasts, and Graves*. Ithaca.

Schwarz, N. 2011. *Thinking Critically about Sorcery and Witchcraft*. Goroka.

Schwoerer, T. 2017. 'Sorcery and Warfare in the Eastern Highlands of Papua New Guinea'. *Oceania* 87.3: 317–36.

Scott, M. W. 2007. *The Severed Snake*. Durham, NC.

Selwyn, G. 1893–4. 'The Islands of the Western Pacific'. *Proceedings of the Royal Colonial Institute, Report* 25: 361–91.

Sharp, N. 1993. *Stars of Tagai*. Canberra.

Shears, R. 1980. *The Coconut War*. Sydney.

   2007. 'The Murdering Messiah'. *Daily Mail.*, dailymail.co.uk/news/ article-439755 (last updated 3 March 2007)

Silas, Brother. 1993. 'Myth and Countermyth in the Siane'. *Melanesian Journal of Theology* 9.2: 63–72.

Sillitoe, P. 2000. *Social Change in Melanesia*. Cambridge.

Sinclair, K. 1961. *The Origins of the Maori Wars*. Oxford.

Sipari, H. 1985. 'The Kopani "Cargo Religion"'. In *New Religious Movements in Melanesia*, eds C. E. Loeliger and G. W. Trompf, 34–9. Suva.

Smith, J. 1998. 'From Cosmos to Nation State: The Shifting of the Yali Worldview' (online: www.academu.edu/21070228/ From_Cosmos_to_Nation_State_The_Shifting_of_the_Yali_Worldvie w_in_Concepts_of_Community_Power_Locus_and_Leadership)

Smith, M. D. (ed.). 2018. *Encyclopedia of Rape and Sexual Violence*, vol. 1. Santa Barbara, CA.

Smith, V. 1998. *Literary Culture and the Pacific*. Cambridge.

Snow, P. and S. Waine. 1979. *The People from the Horizon*. New York.

Souter, G. 1963. *New Guinea – The Last Unknown*. Sydney.

Spate, O. H. K. 2004. *The Spanish Lake*. Canberra.

Spenger, H. 2008. 'Hexerei und Zauberei in Papua-Neuguinea'. In *Pazifik*, ed. F. Kürschner-Pelkmann, 96–101. Hamburg.

Spurway, J. T. 2015. *Ma'afu, Prince of Tonga, Chief of Fiji*. Canberra.

St. Johnston, A. 1889. *Camping among Cannibals*. London.

Stacey, J. J. 2011 'Ordination of Women in the Catholic Church'. (Master's dissertation, University of Sydney, Sydney)

Standish, B. 1999–2000. 'Papua New Guinea 1999'. *Parliament of Australia Research Paper* 4: 1–25 (online: aph.gov.au).

   2003. 'Papua New Guinea's Most Turbulent Election'. *Catalyst* 32.2: 230–48.

Stanmore, Baron A. H.-G. 1879. *Disturbances in the Highland (known as the 'Devil Country') of Viti Levu, Fiji, 1876*, 2 vols. Edinburgh.

Steinbauer, F. 1971. 'Die Cargo-Kulte als religionsgeschichtliches und missionstheolgisches Problem'. (Doctoral dissertation, Universität Erlangen-Nürnberg, Erlangen)

Stewart, C. 2008. 'Men Behaving Badly'. *Journal of Pacific History* 43.1: 77–93.

Stewart, P. J., and A. Strathern. 2002a. *Violence*. London.

    2002b. *Remaking the World*. Washington.

    2004. *Witchcraft, Sorcery, Rumors, and Gossip*. Cambridge.

    2018. *Sacred Revenge in Oceania*. Cambridge.

Stipe, C. E. et al. 1980 'Anthropologists versus Missionaries'. *Current Anthropology* 21.2: 165–79.

Strathern, A. 1993. *Voices of Conflict*. Pittsburgh, PA.

Strathern, A., and P. J. Stewart. 2007. 'Ethnographic Records from the Western Highlands of Ppaua New Guinea'. In *Anthropology's Debt to Missionaries*, eds. L. Plotnicov et al., 151–60. Pittsburgh, PA.

    2011. *Peace-Making and the Imagination*. Brisbane.

Strauss, H., and H. Tischner. (1962) 1990. *The Mi-Culture of the Mount Hagen People*, trans. B. Shields, eds. G. Stürzenhofecker and A. Strathern. Pittsburgh, PA.

Strelan, J. G. 1977. *Search for Salvation*. Adelaide.

Stuebel, O. (ed.) 1895. *Samoanische Texte unter Beihülfe von Eigeborenen*. Berlin.

Sutherland, W. 1908–10. 'The Tuka Religion'. *Transactions of the Fijian Society*: 51–7.

Swain, T. and G. Trompf. 1995. *Religions of Oceania*. London.

Talmon, Y. 1966. 'Millenarian Movements'. *Archive Européennes de Sociologie* 7: 159–200.

Tanggahma, L. 2012. 'A History of the Morning Star Flag in West Papua' (online: westpapuamedia.info).

Tanu, J. 1977. *Rotuma*, ed. C. Plant. Suva.

Ter Harr, G. (ed.). 2005. *Bridge or Barrier*. Leiden.

Terrell, J. E. 1988. *Prehistory in the Pacific Islands*. Cambridge.

Thomas, N. 1990. *Islanders*. New Haven, CN.

Thomson, J. P. 1892. *British New Guinea*. London.

Thomson, P. 2008. *Kava in the Blood*. Charleston, NC.

Thornley, A. 2000. *Exodus of the I Taukei*, with Fijian text, trans. T. Vulaono. Suva.

Timmer, J. 2012. 'Visualizing the Lost Temple and Mapping a Straightening World in Solomon Islands'. In *Handbook of New Religions and Cultural Production*, eds. C. Cusack and A. Norman, 737–52. Leiden.

Toft, S., and S. Bonnell. 1985 *Marriage and Domestic Violence in Rural Papua New Guinea*. Port Moresby.

Tolstoy, L. 1885. *My Religion*, trans. H. Smith. New York.

Tomlinson, M. 2020. *God Is Samoan*. Honolulu, HI.

Tomlinson, M., and D. McDougall (eds.). 2012 *Christian Politics in Oceania*. Oxford.

Tomasetti, F. E. 1976. *Traditionen und Christentum*. Wiesbaden.

Tongamoa, T. (ed.) 1988. *Pacific Women*. Suva.

Trompf, G. W. 1979. 'Man Facing Death and After-Life in Melanesia'. In *Powers, Plumes and Piglets*, ed. N. Habel, 121–36. Adelaide.

    1980. 'Jimmy Stevens, Betrayer of a Faith'. *Pacific Islands Monthly* 51.11: 29–33.

    1983–4. 'Independent Churches of Melanesia'. *Oceania* 54.1–2: 51–72, 122–32.

    1984. 'What Has Happened to Melanesian "Cargo Cults"?' In *Religious Movements in Melanesia Today*, ed. W. Flannery, 29–51. Goroka.

    1988. 'Melanesian Religion in All Its Aspects'. *Catalyst* 18.2: 155–62.

1989a. 'Doesn't Colonialism Make You Mad?' In *Papua New Guinea: A Century of Colonial Impact, 1884–1984*, ed. S. Latukefu, 247–77. Port Moresby.

1989b. 'Konkurrierende Wertevorstellungen'. In *Papua-Neuguinea*, eds. H. Wagner et al., 314–24. Neuendettelsau.

(ed.). 1990. *Cargo Cults and Millenarian Movements*. Berlin.

1994. 'Gangs and Politics'. *Current Affairs Bulletin* 71.2: 32–7.

1996. 'Gang Leaders and Conversion in Contemporary Papua New Guinea'. In *Religious Change, Conversion and Culture*, ed. L. Olson, 209–25. Sydney.

1997. 'La logica della ritorsione e lo studio delle religioni della Melanesia'. *Religioni e Società* 12.28: 48–72.

2000. 'On the Edge of Asia'. In *The Asian Church in the New Millennium*, ed. R. Fernández-Calienes, 30–60. Delhi.

2003. 'On Wondering about Wonder: Melanesians and the Cargo'. In *Beyond Primitivism*, ed. J. Olupona), 297–313. New York.

2004. *Melanesian Religion*. Cambridge.

2005. *In Search of Origins*. Slough, UK.

2006. *Religions of Melanesia*. London.

2007. 'Of Colligation and Reification in the Representation of Religion and Violence'. In *Ecumenics from the Rim*, eds. J. O'Grady and P. Scherle, 179–86. Berlin.

2008a. *Payback*. Cambridge.

2008b. 'Indigenous Religions'. In *Christian Approaches to Other Faiths*, eds A. Race and P. Hedges, 290–307. London.

2011. 'Pacific Millennial Movements'. In *The Oxford Handbook of Millennialism*, ed. C. Wessinger, 436–53. Oxford.

2015. 'New Religious Movements in Oceania'. *Nova Religio* 18.4: 6–12.

2018. 'Independent Churches'. In *Encyclopedia of Christianity in the Global South*, ed. M. A. Lamport, vol. 1, 367–9. New York.

2020a. 'Cargo Cults'. In *Sage Encyclopedia of the Sociology of Religion*, eds. A. Possamai and A. J. Blasi, vol. 1, 109–10. London.

2020b. 'Melanesians and the Cargo'. In *With This Root about My Person: Charles Long*, eds. J. Reid and D. Carrasco, 63–74. Albuquerque, NM.

2021a. *Violence in Pacific Islander Traditional Religions*. Cambridge.

2021b. 'Rituals Surrounding Sorcery and Witchcraft in Traditional Societies'. In *Palgrave Handbook of Anthropological Ritual Studies*, eds. P. J. Stewart and A. Strathern. New York.

n.d. 'Towards an Understanding of Bougainvillean Nationalism: A Collection of Materials for Limited Circulation'. (Trompf archives, University of Sydney, Sydney)

Trompf, G. W. and F. Tomasetti (eds.). 2023. *Integral Work*. Sydney.

Trompf, R. R. 1985. 'Clinical Notes'. (Unpublished notes, Laloki National Psychiatric Hospital, Port Moresby)

Turner, H. W. 1978. 'The Hidden Power of the Whites'. *Archives de Sciences Sociales des Religions* 46.1: 41–65.

Turner, M. 1990. *Papua New Guinea*. Melbourne.

Urame, J. 2008. 'Media Reports and Public Opinion on Sorcery and Witchcraft in Papua New Guinea'. In *Sorcery, Witchcraft and Christianity in Melanesia*, eds F. Zocca and J. Urame, 67–93. Goroka.

Utrecht, E. 1978. *Papoeas in opstand*. Rotterdam.

Valencia, A. 1891. 'Memória de las Islas de Palaos'. (Typescript M. de la Hoz [1940], MAR Center, University of Guam, Mangilao)

Waiko, J. D. 1970. 'A Payback Murder'. *Journal of the Papua and New Guinea Society* 4.2: 24–35; 67–8.

1976. 'Emboga'. (Unpublished typescript, UPNG, Port Moresby)

Wardlow, H. 2019. 'With AIDS I Am Happier than I Have Ever Been Before'. *The Australian Journal of Anthropology* 30.1: 53–67.

Warry, W. 1987. *Chuave Politicss*. Canberra.

Wassmann, J. (ed.). 1998. *Pacific Answers to Western Hegemony*. Oxford.

Webster, E. 1984. *The Moon Man*. Melbourne.

Webster, P. 1979. *Rua and the Maori Millennium*. Wellington.

Westervelt, W. D. (1915) 1985. *Hawaiian Legends of Ghosts and Ghost Gods*. London. (1915 edn. with different title, *Hawaiian Legends of Gods and Ghosts*)

Wete, P. 1991. '*Agis ou moeurs*'. Suva.

Whiteman, D. 2002. *Melanesians and Missionaries*. Eugene, OR.

Whiting, N., and B. Harriman. 2019. 'The Murder of a PNG Woman sparks National Outcry over Domestic Violence'. *ABC News*, 30 Nov. online: www.abc.net.au/news

Wiessner, P., and N. Pupu. 2012. 'Toward Peace: Indigenous Institutions and Foreign Arms in a Papua New Guinea Society'. *Science* 237.6101: 1651–4.

Wilkes, A. 2019. *Honour, Mana, and Agency in Polynesian-European Conflict*. New York.

Williams, F. E. 1923. *The Vailala Madness and the Destruction of Native Ceremonies in the Gulf Division*. Port Moresby.

    1941. *Natives of Lake Kutubu*. Sydney.

Williams, T. 1858. *Fiji and the Fijians*, ed. G. S. Rowe), vol. 1. London.

Wilson, B. 1973. *Magic and the Millennium*. New York.

Wilson, C. 2018. 'The New Battle for Bougainville's Panguna Mine'. *The Interpreter*, 21 Aug. (online: lowyinstitute.org)

Wilson, M. 2016. *Angel of Kokoda*. Sydney.

Wing, J., and P. King (eds.). 2005. *Genocide in West Papua?* Sydney.

Winks, R. W. 1953. 'The Doctrine of Hau-Hauism'. *Journal of the Polynesian Society* 62.3: 199–236.

Worsley, P. 1970. *The Trumpet Shall Sound*. London.

Yagas, A. 1985. 'The Begesin Rebellion and the Kein "Independence" Movement'.In *New Religious Movements*, eds. C. Loeliger and G. W. Trompf, 18–25. Suva.

Young, Bishop D. 1986. 'Pastoral Responses to Tribal Fighting in Enga'. *Catalyst* 16.1: 7–16.

Zelenietz, M. 1979. 'The Effects of Sorcery in Kilenge, West New Britain Province'. *Law Reform Commission Occasional Paper 11*, Port Moresby.

Zelenietz, M., and S. Lindenbaum (eds.). 1981. *Sorcery and Social Change in Melanesia*. Special issue of *Social Analysis* 8: 1–136.

Zocca, F. 2009. 'Witchcraft and Christianity in Simbu Province'. In *Sanguma in Paradise: Sorcery, Witchcraft and Christianity in Papua New Guinea*,; ed. F. Zocca, 10–54. Goroka.

Please Note: Section 2.2 was developed from a video lecture I gave on 'Violence and Millenarian Cargo Cults' for The Centre for the Critical Study of Apocalyptic and Millenarian Movements (CENSAMM), hosted by Bedford University, 8 May 2017 (online: YouTube), and 2.3 from a lecture on 'Religion and the Management of Conflict in Melanesia' delivered at the University of Papua New Guinea (UPNG), 15 Sept. 2001.

Acknowledgements

For general advice about this Element I express my gratitude to Pamela Stewart and Andrew Strathern, and for help with special points I thank Michael Avosa, hermit Wendy Bartlett, Ben Bohane, Marcus Campbell, John Connell, Paul D'Arcy, Sinclair Dinnen, Julian Droogan, Jon Fraenkel, Patrick Gesch, Michael Goldsmith, Anna-Karina Hermkens, Francis Hezel, Rose Kinney, Carl Loeliger, 'David' Teng Yueh Ma, Ennio Mantovani, John D'Arcy May, Grant McCall, Glen Petersen, Alexander Polunin, Christopher Rowland, John Shaver, Jukka Siikala, (the late) Bill Standish, Jaap Timmer, (the late) Friedegard Tomasetti, Terence Wesley-Smith, Tigger Wise, Richard Udy and Douglas Young. Once again I honour the series editors Margo Kitts and the late James Lewis, with both Beatrice Rehl and Vibhu Prathima Palanisame of Cambridge University Press, for their encouragement and patience; and for looking after my welfare, how crucial has been my wife, dearest Izabella! As for this small tome's dedication, it is to treasured dear-departed friends, whose presence in my life I sorely miss: Fr Dr Zymunt ('Ziggy') Kruzcek, intrepid researcher in the history of churches in Oceania, and Jenny Mek, skilled broadcaster and fellow researcher into Papua New Guinea Highland women's affairs.

Cambridge Elements ☰

Religion and Violence

FOUNDING EDITOR
†James R. Lewis
Wuhan University

James R. Lewis was Professor at Wuhan University, and the author and editor of a number of volumes, including *The Cambridge Companion to Religion and Terrorism.*

SERIES EDITOR
Margo Kitts
Hawai'i Pacific University

Margo Kitts edits the *Journal of Religion and Violence* and is Professor and Coordinator of Religious Studies and East-West Classical Studies at Hawai'i Pacific University in Honolulu.

ABOUT THE SERIES
Violence motivated by religious beliefs has become all too common in the years since the 9/11 attacks. Not surprisingly, interest in the topic of religion and violence has grown substantially since then. This Elements series on Religion and Violence addresses this new, frontier topic in a series of ca. fifty individual Elements. Collectively, the volumes will examine a range of topics, including violence in major world religious traditions, theories of religion and violence, holy war, witch-hunting, and human sacrifice, among others.

Cambridge Elements⁼

Religion and Violence

Printed in the United States
by Baker & Taylor Publisher Services